ALSO BY EVAN OSNOS

Age of Ambition:
Chasing Fortune, Truth, and Faith
in the New China

JOE BIDEN

The LIFE, *the* RUN, *and*
WHAT MATTERS NOW

EVAN OSNOS

SCRIBNER

New York   London   Toronto   Sydney   New Delhi

Scribner

An Imprint of Simon & Schuster, Inc.

1230 Avenue of the Americas

New York, NY 10020

For information about special discounts for bulk purchases, please contact Simon & Schuster Special Sales at 1-866-506-1949 or business@simonandschuster.com.

The Simon & Schuster Speakers Bureau can bring authors to your live event. For more information, or to book an event, contact the Simon & Schuster Speakers Bureau at 1-866-248-3049 or visit our website at www.simonspeakers.com.

Manufactured in the United States of America

1 3 5 7 9 10 8 6 4 2

Library of Congress Cataloging-in-Publication Data has been applied for.

ISBN 978-1-9821-7402-6
ISBN 978-1-9821-7409-5 (ebook)

For my mother, Susan, who taught me to read;
and, for my father, Peter, who taught me to write.

People pay for what they do, and, still more,
for what they have allowed themselves to become.
And they pay for it very simply: by the lives they lead.

—James Baldwin, *No Name in the Street*

But I am bound upon a wheel of fire,
That mine own tears do scald like molten lead.

—Shakespeare, *King Lear*

Contents

JOE BIDEN

Prologue

February 12, 1988

A forty-five-year-old man—white male, father of three—awoke on the floor of his hotel room. He had been unconscious for five hours. He could barely move his legs. He did not know how he got there. He remembered only a flash of agony; he had given a speech in Rochester, New York, and returned to his room, where he felt a sensation akin to a cleaver parting his skull. For months, he had ignored a strange ache in his head and neck, burying it in Tylenol, blaming it on the ludicrous rigor of running for president while heading the Judiciary Committee of the United States Senate. The campaign had ended in embarrassment—a product of his own arrogance, he admitted to himself—but the headaches had continued.

The man heaved himself onto the bed. From there, his assistant got him to a plane to Delaware, where doctors identified a cranial aneurysm, the ballooning of an artery that fed the brain. His prospects for survival were so grim that a priest was summoned to deliver last rites, even before the man's wife could be there. In the hours that followed, he was rushed through the slanting snow of a storm to Washington, D.C., where a surgeon warned that the operation might rob him of the ability to speak. "I kind of wish that had happened last summer," the man replied.

For three months, through more surgery, more complications, he was supine, confined to a hospital bed. Oddly enough, his failure in the presidential campaign had probably saved his life. Had he stayed on the road, crisscrossing New Hampshire and ignoring his symptoms, he might not be there at all. In the depth of his ordeal, a doctor turned to him and said he was a "lucky man." Seven months passed before the man could get back up and return to work. He told the first crowd he saw that he had been given a "second chance in life."

More than thirty years after Joe Biden nearly died on his back, the moment is often lost amid the official milestones of his political biography. But that instant contains the defining pattern of his life—a journey of improbable turns, some spectacularly fortunate and others almost inconceivably cruel. Biden's ambition to reach the highest rungs of American power has driven his rise for more than five decades. When he was barely out of his teens, the mother of a girlfriend (later, his first wife, Neilia Hunter) asked about his professional goals. "President," Biden said, and added, "of the United States."

His political career placed him at pivotal moments of modern American history, including some of the nation's defining conflicts around race, gender, crime, health, capitalism, and warfare. He made mistakes, explained himself, and paid a price. Time and again, he defied predictions that he was finished—only to find himself, to his astonishment, beside Barack Obama, in a historic run for the White House. In his speech at the 2008 Democratic National Convention, he said, "Failure at some point in your life is inevitable, but giving up is unforgivable."

In the vice presidency—the most maligned job in Washington—Biden often projected the look of a man who couldn't quite believe his good fortune. The trials of his life had relieved him of some solemn self-regard. A British minister once asked him, in a private meeting, for the protocol in addressing one another. Biden gave a theatrical glance to either side, and said, "It looks like we're alone, so why don't you call me Mr. President and I'll call you Mr. Prime Minister."

By 2020, he was a political veteran marked by so many years and battles that his opponents, and even some of his admirers, questioned the wisdom of yet one more race. And, then, he foiled the predictions once more, emerging as the Democratic nominee for president in a showdown of such grave implication for America's future that it made a mockery of the usual clichés about the most important election in our lifetime. He was in a one-on-one contest against Donald Trump for an office that was losing its stature as the leader of the free world.

The circumstances of a life in full and a country in peril conspired to put Joe Biden at the center of an American reckoning, prompting an urgent appetite, at home and abroad, to divine what had made him, how he thought, what he carried, and what he lacked. At the very moment that his country was lying spread-eagled before the eyes of the world, Biden had arrived at his season of history.

CHAPTER 1

Annus Horribilis

The lush, well-to-do Wilmington suburbs, in the rolling woods of the Brandywine Valley, are popular with heirs to the chemical fortune of the du Pont family. Their estates and gardens are tucked away in what is known as Delaware's Chateau Country. On a modest patch, by those standards, Joe Biden and his wife, Jill, live on four sloping acres that overlook a small lake.

On the ninety-ninth day before the election, I pulled into Biden's driveway. To avoid contagion, his advisers put me in a carriage house, a hundred yards from the home where the family lives. "Welcome to my mom's house," Biden called from the bottom of the stairs, an instant before his sweep of white hair rose into view. He reached the second floor of the cottage. He wore a trim blue dress shirt, sleeves rolled to the elbows, a pen tucked between the buttons, and a bright-white N95 mask.

Biden was three weeks away from becoming America's Democratic nominee for president. The headline on the front page of *The Washington Post* that morning was "America's Standing in the World Is at a Low Ebb." The death toll from the coronavirus pandemic was approaching 150,000, three times as many lives as America lost in Vietnam; the economy had crumbled faster than at any other time in the nation's history; in Portland, Oregon, federal agents in unmarked uniforms were tear-gassing protesters, whom Donald Trump called "sick and deranged Anarchists & Agitators." On Twitter that day, Trump warned that the demonstrators would "destroy our American cities, and worse, if Sleepy Joe Biden, the puppet of the Left, ever won. Markets would crash and cities would burn."

The man who stood between Americans and four more years of Trump looked pleased to have company. In the strange summer of 2020, the Biden place was as solemn and secluded as an abbey. The cottage, styled in Celtic themes (green shutters, a thistle pattern on the throw pillows), doubled as a command post for the Secret Service, and large men with holstered guns stalked in and out. Biden settled into an armchair across the room from me and splayed his hands, a socially distanced salute. "The docs keep it really tight," he explained.

Later that afternoon, the Bidens were due on Capitol Hill, to pay their respects to the recently deceased

John Lewis, of Georgia, a civil rights icon who endured a fractured skull at the hands of state troopers in Selma, Alabama, before rising to the House of Representatives and becoming known as the "conscience of Congress." It would be a rare excursion. Since the Covid-19 shutdown began, in March, Biden had circulated mostly between his back porch, where he convened fund-raisers on Zoom, a gym upstairs, and the basement rec room, where he sat for TV interviews in front of a bookcase and a folded flag. The campaign apparatus had scattered into the homes of some twenty-three hundred employees.

Before I could ask a question, he explained the origins of the cottage. When his father, Joe Sr., fell ill, in 2002, Biden renovated the basement of the main house and moved his parents in. "God love him, he lasted for about six months," he said. "I thought my mom would stay." She had other ideas. (Biden's late mother, the former Jean Finnegan, plays a formidable role in his recounting of family history. In grammar school, he recalls, a nun mocked him for stuttering, and his mother, a devout Catholic, told her, "If you ever speak to my son like that again, I'll come back and rip that bonnet off your head.")

After Jean became a widow, Biden said, she offered him a proposition: "She said, 'Joey, if you build me a house, I'll move in here.' I said, 'Honey, I don't have the money to build you a house.' She said, 'I know you don't.' She said, 'But I talked to your brothers and sister. Sell my house and build me an apartment.'" For years, Biden, who relied on his government salary, was among the least prosperous members of the United States Senate. (In the two years after he left the vice presidency, the Bidens earned more than $15 million, from speeches, teaching, and book deals.) Biden renovated an old garage and his mother moved in. "I'd walk in and she'd be in that chair downstairs, facing the fireplace, watching television," he said. "There'd always be a caregiver on the stool, and she'd be hearing her confession."

Joe Biden has been a "public man," as he puts it— holding office, giving interviews, dispensing anecdotes— for five decades. I last interviewed him, mostly about foreign affairs, in 2014, when he was in the White House and Donald Trump was hosting Season 14 of *The Apprentice*. Biden is seventy-seven years old, and he looks thinner than he did six years ago, but not markedly so. He has parted with youth grudgingly. His smile has been rejuvenated to such a gleam that it inspired a popular tweet during the 2012 campaign: "Biden's teeth are so white they're voting for Romney." His hairline has been reforested, his forehead appears becalmed, and Biden generally projects the glow of a grandfather just back from the gym, which is often the case. His verbiage is as meandering as ever. James Comey, the former FBI direc-

tor, once wrote that the typical Biden conversation originated in "Direction A" before "heading in Direction Z."
(In December 2019, Biden's campaign released a doctor's
summary of his medical records, which pronounced him
a "healthy, vigorous" man of his age.)

The implications of age, in one form or another, hov-
ered over the presidential race. Trump took office as the
oldest president in history. By the summer of 2020, he
was seventy-four. To deflect questions about his mental
acuity, he and his allies presented Biden as senile, a theme
that dominated right-wing TV and Twitter. Biden saw
little of it; he didn't look at social media. (Compared to
Trump, Biden's campaign made only perfunctory use of
it. Trump had over 114 million combined followers on
Twitter and Facebook; Biden has less than ten million.)

If there is something big, his staff included a tweet in
the morning roundup of news that he read on his phone.
But, he said, "I don't look at a lot of the comments. I
spend the time trying to focus on the trouble people are
in right now."

By the end of August, ten weeks before the election,
Biden led Trump by an average of at least 8 percentage
points. But no earthly inhabitant expected an ordinary
end to the campaign. Some polls showed the race tight-
ening, and it could be transformed by a sudden jolt in the
economy or in Congress or the Supreme Court. "I feel

good about where we are," Biden said. "But I know that it's going to get really, really ugly." As Trump disputed the legitimacy of mail-in voting, his postmaster general was brazenly cutting service in ways that could prevent ballots from being counted. Ruth Bader Ginsburg, the oldest Supreme Court justice, had recently begun chemotherapy, raising the prospects of a bitter partisan fight over a successor. Republican operatives were helping Kanye West, the pro-Trump hip-hop star, get on the ballot in multiple states, which critics suspected would siphon away Black votes from Biden. Meanwhile, U.S. intelligence warned that, as in 2016, Russians were working to damage Trump's opponent, this time with phone recordings edited to support the canard that Biden had used the vice presidency to help his son Hunter make money in Ukraine.

For a front-runner, Biden was hardly sanguine. "I am worried about them screwing around with the election outcome," he said. "When the hell have you heard a president say, 'I'm not sure I'll accept the outcome'?"

The trials of 2020 dismantled some of the most basic stories we Americans tell ourselves. The world's richest, most powerful country botched even rudimentary responses to the pandemic—finding masks, making tests—and some agencies proved to be so antiquated and starved of resources that they used fax machines to share data. The White House offered policies that read like mock Kafka; even as people were advised against dining out, it was proposing a corporate tax break on business meals.

Unlike World War II, when middle-class Americans skimped on basic staples—meat, sugar, coffee—many Americans of the Covid-19 era had rejected appeals to stay at home or cover their faces. Some ventured out on spring break, while stock clerks, nursing home aides, and delivery personnel returned to work under orders that they were "essential." In Washington, even basic standards of political cohesion were failing. When Larry Hogan, of Maryland, a Republican governor at odds with Trump, ordered test kits from South Korea, Hogan felt the need to deploy his state police and National Guard troops to protect the shipment, for fear that the federal government would try to seize it. Trump boasted that he had withheld aid and equipment to states with Democratic leaders. "Don't call the governor of Washington," he recalled telling his vice president, Mike Pence. "Don't call the woman in Michigan." On Fox News in April, Jared Kushner, the president's son-in-law and one of the leaders of the coronavirus response, declared the administration's effort "a great success story." In the four months afterward, at least 110,000 more people died.

And, in the midst of the pandemic, the death of George Floyd under a policeman's knee opened a second epochal turn in American history—a reckoning with the entrenched hierarchy of power, which Isabel Wilkerson, in her book *Caste*, called "the wordless usher in a darkened theater, flashlight cast down in the aisles, guiding us to our assigned seats."

Cornell William Brooks, a Harvard professor, an activist, and a former head of the NAACP, likened the killing of George Floyd to the murder of Emmett Till in 1955, which inspired the Montgomery movement for civil rights. The scale of the protests reflected a rage that ran deeper than the horror that incited it. "The hottest element in this cauldron is frustrated hope. Many of us remember 'hope and change,' and what we got in the wake of that was literally anger and fear. People have just had enough," Brooks said.

Biden believed that Trump's failures of leadership, particularly in the pandemic, had become clear even to steadfast Republican advocates. "Everybody knows, even people supporting him: this is all about his self-interest. It's all about him," he told me. "It has had profound impacts on people's ability to live their life." Still, he conceded, it might not suffice to change voters' minds. When Biden characterized Trump's supporters, they were not duped or culpable or deplorable. "They think that they will be materially better off if he's president," he said. "He has gotten through, I think, to some degree—to about 40 percent—saying, 'The Democrats are socialists. They're here to take away everything you have.'"

Republicans had long accused Democrats of plotting to smuggle socialism into the United States. But leveling that charge against Biden, whose career had been distinguished mostly by careful centrism, was an awkward task. Biden entered the Democratic primaries with a narrow goal: to end the Trump presidency. Most Americans, he argued, did not want a revolution. At an early fund-raiser in New York, he promised not to "demonize" the rich and said that "nothing would fundamentally change." (Online, people circulated mock campaign posters, in the color-block style of Obama's "Hope" picture, with the slogan "Nothing Would Fundamentally Change.") But, by the time Biden effectively clinched the nomination, in March, he had begun to describe his candidacy as a bid for systemic change on the scale of Franklin Roosevelt's New Deal. According to a senior aide to Bernie Sanders, Biden told Sanders, in a phone call about a possible endorsement, "I want to be the most progressive president since FDR."

That evolution confounded critics on all sides. Biden was simultaneously accused of being a socialist puppet and a neoliberal shill. To his detractors on the left—especially younger, highly educated, more ideological Democrats who are particularly active online—Biden was a creature of the ancien régime and a cheerleader of the national security state, with such timid appetites for change that, when he won on Super Tuesday, the price of health care stocks went up. Liberals were dismayed that the most diverse presidential field in history had yielded a white man in his eighth decade. It was as if a waiter had returned from the kitchen with news that the specials were gone, and all that was left was oatmeal. (Of course, they always had the option of more rat poison.)

Maurice Mitchell, the national director of the Working Families Party, told me, "People said, 'Oh, this man's a hack.' He's not an ideological person, and ideology clearly matters to us. He was running a retrograde candidacy during the primary. It was all about going back to the track we were on with the Obama years." Mitchell, who was also a leader in the Movement for Black Lives, said that Biden's change of tone caught the attention of progressives: "He's recognizing that this might be a Rooseveltian moment. He's not all the way there—nobody thinks Joe Biden is a progressive star—but he can be a product of either your most cynical thinking or a product of your most optimistic thinking."

In an interview as the election approached, I asked Barack Obama how he interpreted Biden's swerve to the left. "If you look at Joe Biden's goals and Bernie Sanders's goals, they're not that different, from a forty-thousand-foot level," he argued. "They both want to make sure everybody has health care. They want to make sure everybody can get a job that pays a living wage. They want to make sure every child gets a good education." The question was one of tactics, Obama suggested. "A lot of times, the issue has to do with 'How do we go about that, and what are the coalitions we need?'" he said. "What I think the moment has done is to change some of those calculations, not because necessarily Joe's changed but because circumstances have changed."

The tensions afflicting the Democratic Party reflected a clash between liberal meliorism—the "long-view" politics of Obama and Biden—and the urgent movement that Sanders called a "revolution." The two factions claim competing virtues: one emphasized realism, coalition-building, and practical politics, and the other the inescapable evidence that regular "reform" had failed to confront pervasive inequalities, the cruelties of American health care and incarceration, and ecological catastrophe.

The division was as much generational as it was ideological. Young Americans have been reared on fiascoes—the invasion of Iraq, the response to Hurricane Katrina, the 2008 financial crisis—and have come to blame that record partly on gerontocracy. The median American age in 2020 was thirty-eight years. The median U.S. senator was sixty-five. The current Congress was among the oldest in history. Senate Majority Leader Mitch McConnell was seventy-eight; House Speaker Nancy Pelosi was eighty. The difference in age was at the root of a profound difference in worldview. In the words of Patrick Fisher, a Seton Hall professor who specializes in the political dynamics of age, "Demographically, politically, economically, socially and technologically, the generations are more different from each other now than at any time in living memory."

Millennials constitute the largest generation in America today, and the most diverse in the nation's history. They entered the job market during the worst recession since the 1930s. People under twenty-five have faced unemployment rates more than double those of other age groups. By 2012, a record number of adults between eighteen and thirty-one were living with their parents. In the 2010s, as Trumpism was germinating on the right, a rival political movement was growing on the left, driven by young people. In their view, older Americans were using the political system to steer resources away from younger generations. In 2014, the federal government spent approximately six dollars per capita on programs for seniors for every dollar that it spent on programs for children, according to Paul Taylor, the author of *The Next America*, a study of the demographic future.

Many young Americans had put their hopes in Obama; in 2008, he won an astonishing two thirds of millennials. By the end of his term, they had concluded that if he could not marshal political parties to act then nobody could. Between 2013 and 2017, the median age of members of the Democratic Socialists of America dropped from sixty-eight to thirty-three. Many others expressed a desire for a socialism that was closer to the New Deal. In 2019, Greta Thunberg, the Swedish teenager who inspired a global climate strike, told the United Nations, "Change is coming, whether you like it or not."

When I asked Obama about the tensions in the party, he cast them as features of "the traditional Democratic idea." He said, "You have a big-tent party. And that means that you tolerate, listen to, and embrace folks who are different than you, and try to get them in the fold. And so you work with not just liberal Democrats, but you work with conservative Democrats—and you are willing to compromise on issues." That was a gentle jab at Democrats who see compromise as a failing. In comments the previous year, Obama bemoaned the emergence of a "circular firing squad" in the party. "This idea of purity, and you're never compromised, and you're always politically woke, and all that stuff, you should get over that quickly," he said.

Before he was a candidate, Biden expressed frustration with young people's tepid participation in elections. In 2019, he griped that, when Trump ran against Hillary Clinton, "they sat home, didn't get involved." Yet, when we spoke during his campaign, he took pains to sound more conciliatory. "This generation has really been screwed," he said. "These were really the most open, the least prejudiced, the brightest, the best-educated generation in American history. And what's happening? They end up with 9/11, they end up with a war, they end up with the Great Recession, and then they end up with this. This generation deserves help in the middle of this crisis." He understood elements of their predicament. "I'm paying off Beau Biden's college loans," he said, referring to his firstborn son, who died in 2015. "He never missed a payment, but when he graduated from undergraduate school and law school, it was $124,000 he owed."

In the spring of 2020, Biden began describing himself as a "transition candidate," explaining, "We have not given a bench to younger people in the party, the opportunity to have the focus and be in focus for the rest of the country. There's an incredible group of talented, newer, younger people." Ben Rhodes, an adviser to Obama in the White House, told me, "It's actually a really powerful idea. It says, 'I'm a seventy-seven-year-old white man, who was a senator for thirty years, and I understand both those limitations and the nature of this country.' Because, no matter what he does, he cannot completely understand the frustration of people in the streets. That's not a criticism. It's just a reality." A senior Obama administration official observed that Biden's acknowledgment also contained a subtler message: "This country needs to just chill the fuck out and have a boring president."

To Varshini Prakash, a twenty-seven-year-old co-founder of the Sunrise Movement, a youth-driven organization that presses for action on climate change, Biden recognized the urgency of showing more than rhetorical interest in the young left. "You have a presidential candidate who essentially staked his career on advocating incremental solutions," she told me. "Then he finds himself at this moment where people are fed up with much of the status quo he represents—an economic system that has reigned supreme for forty years, that he was part of advocating for, but also health, climate, gun violence, immigration. All of these have reached a fever pitch. I think Covid-19 was the moment that pushed it over the edge, where he recognized if he doesn't have a way to meet his incrementalism with the level of transformative change that people are crying out for, he's going to be in deep trouble."

• • •

For the ride to Lewis's memorial, Biden boarded an armored black SUV. He had changed from campaign-from-home attire into mourning clothes—a crisp white shirt, dark suit and tie, and black mask. At the Capitol Rotunda, he and Jill were met by Nancy Pelosi, whom they hadn't seen since the lockdowns began. They huddled in conversation, and then the Bidens approached Lewis's flag-draped casket, which rested on the spot where Abraham Lincoln lay in state, a century and a half ago. Like others, Biden had challenged Republicans to honor Lewis by restoring the Voting Rights Act—to "protect the sacred right to vote that he was willing to die for," as Biden put it. The law had served as a check on racial discrimination at the polls from 1965 to 2013, when the Supreme Court ruled that conditions no longer required it. Since then, Republicans in many states have expanded efforts to bar voters through specious requirements; in the Senate, McConnell has blocked bills seeking to restore the act.

Biden had spoken to Lewis for the last time by phone a few days before he died. When the news of his death arrived he wrote in a statement for the press: "For parents trying to answer their children's questions about what to make of the world we are in today, teach them about John Lewis."

In the days afterward, Lewis's casket retraced an arc of the Black freedom struggle, beginning in his hometown of Troy, Alabama, crossing the Edmund Pettus Bridge, in Selma, and stopping at the newly christened Black Lives Matter Plaza, near the White House. At the Capitol, Biden laid his hand on the casket and made the sign of the cross.

Trump, for his part, skipped the tribute. Lewis once declared that he was not a "legitimate president," to which Trump responded, in an unsubtle slur, that Lewis's congressional district was "crime infested." Under pressure to say something, Trump had tweeted, on the way back from golf, that he was saddened, and that "Melania and I send our prayers to he and his family."

In the presidential race, the upheavals of 2020 have afforded Trump abundant opportunities to look racist and inept, while sparing Biden, a famously loose-lipped campaigner, the risks of slogging through a full schedule. His aides disputed suggestions that they have been purposely allowing Trump to hog the spotlight, but, in May, Biden said frankly, "The more he talks, the better off I am."

Reticence has never been Biden's default mode. Even in Washington, the windbag Mecca, he distinguished himself. When Obama, newly arrived in the Senate in 2005, heard Biden hold forth in a meeting of the Foreign Relations Committee, he passed an aide a three-word note: "Shoot. Me. Now." A former longtime staffer recalled that he learned to flex his knees during the boss's speeches to avoid fainting. Biden knows his reputation and sometimes jokes about it. When his microphone once malfunctioned during a television interview, he said, "They do this to me at the White House all the time."

Biden's conspicuous appetite for human connection was likely a big factor in his primary victory. The former mayor of South Bend, Indiana, Pete Buttigieg, one of his opponents, observed Biden backstage before a debate. "Some candidates would be talking to each other," he told me. "Some candidates would be talking almost to themselves." But Biden was kibbitzing with the stage-hands or trying to buck up the newcomer candidates. "I think any human being who's around is somebody that he's equally happy to engage and talk to and listen to."

As the election loomed, Biden faced a predicament: his political success had never come from soaring speeches or the clever use of social media; it came from reaching people—and the pandemic had made people almost impossible to reach. The question was whether he could make connections with enough voters to beat Trump, when many Democrats would have preferred another Democratic nominee.

CHAPTER 2

What It Took

B iden vacillates between embracing the image of a kindly grandfather and bristling at it. The late-night host Stephen Colbert once referred to him on the air as a "nice old man." It was 2015, and Biden called him the next day, Colbert told me. "He goes, 'Listen, buddy, you call me a nice old man one more time and I will personally come down there and kick your ass.' I laughed, and he laughed. I said, 'Don't worry. I won't call you a nice old man, because clearly you're not *that* nice.'"

In truth, Biden's effusiveness has always accompanied a prickly side. Among staff, he is known for giving support to talented people without connections, and calling his employees' mothers as a surprise, but he can also be curt and demanding, leaving the menial work of fundraising to others. He sometimes lavishes more gratitude on strangers who want selfies than on aides who have spent years keeping him in office. Jeff Connaughton, a disenchanted former aide, once called Biden an "egomaniacal autocrat." But Connaughton, who became a lobbyist, also admired Biden's contempt for the corrupting glad-handing of Washington. "Biden never lifted a finger for me or for one of my clients," he wrote, in his book, *The Payoff*. "Unlike most of Congress, he hardly ever schmoozed with the Permanent Class. He did the best he could to stay as far away from it as possible."

For all his longevity in Washington, Biden has never quite belonged to the technocratic elite. To the dominant Democrats—the Clinton and Obama circles—he was too mawkish with the Amtrak Joe routine, too transparent in his ambition. Biden is the first Democratic nominee without an Ivy League degree since Walter Mondale, in 1984. In a milieu of Rhodes Scholars and former professors, he is thin-skinned about condescension, real and imagined. He was barely in the West Wing before *The Onion* declared, in a headline, "Shirtless Biden Washes Trans Am in White House Driveway," establishing a theme—"Amtrak Joe," the hell-raiser at the end of the bar—that was so enduring that it obscured the fact that he is a lifelong teetotaler. (Too many alcoholics in his family, he said. He grew up sharing a room with his mother's brother, and recalled of the experience, "Even as kids, we noticed Uncle Boo-Boo drank a bit heavily.")

Biden's insecurities fed a certain openness and vulnerability. Even after decades in national office, he talked to anyone in reach, partly because he was trawling for what others knew and he did not. A senior Obama administration official, who periodically briefed Biden, recalled, "He would talk for 90 percent of the conversation. And yet he always picked something up. At the end, we'd get up and walk out, and he'd clap me on the back: 'Great talk.' And I'd be a bit dazed." The official added, "So the question is which Joe Biden governs: The one that is sincerely open and searching for the perspectives that will help him be more effective? Or the Joe Biden that will talk at you because he thinks he has enough words and expertise to muscle through any situation?"

For years, Biden has contended with a harrowing tendency to put his foot in his mouth. Talking about American soldiers who were hounded by debt collectors during deployments, he once condemned the "Shylocks who took advantage of these women and men." In footage of the speech, in the fall of 2014, his gaze swept across the audience, and, judging from the flicker that passed across his face, one senses that he glimpsed a familiar hint that he may have devoured another heaping portion of foot. "Action is eloquence," Shakespeare observed, in the early 1600s, just a few years after he wrote *The Merchant of Ven-*

ice, the play that established a Shylock as a reliable slur. After Biden's comment, the Anti-Defamation League's national director, Abraham Foxman, said it remained "an offensive characterization to this day." Because Biden is a longtime supporter of the Jewish community, Foxman put the moment in context: "When someone as friendly to the Jewish community, and as open and tolerant an individual as is Vice President Joe Biden, uses the term 'Shylocked' to describe unscrupulous money lenders dealing with service men and women, we see once again how deeply embedded this stereotype about Jews is in society." (Biden quickly apologized for "a poor choice of words.")

A few weeks later, he was in trouble again—but, this time, it was for saying something true. At Harvard's Kennedy School, Biden finished his formal remarks and went free range when a student asked whether the U.S. should have intervened earlier in the Syrian civil war. "Our allies in the region were our largest problem in Syria," Biden said, a characterization that allies do not generally enjoy. He listed the Turks, the Saudis, and the Emiratis, and said, "They poured hundreds of millions of dollars and tens of tons of weapons into anyone who would fight against Assad—except that the people who were being supplied were Al Nusra, and Al Qaeda," a stream of support that helped foster a resurgence in Sunni radicalism.

Turkish president Recep Tayyip Erdoğan demanded an apology and called his relationship with Biden "history." (Biden apologized to Erdoğan two days later.)

His tendency to say out loud what others in Washington said in private caused him trouble at work. In describing the role of America's regional allies in Syria, Biden was largely correct. The U.S. had publicly called on the Turks to seal their border to jihadists en route to Syria, and experts did not question that money from Gulf countries had ended up in the hands of militant extremists there. Andrew J. Tabler, of the Washington Institute for Near East Policy, told *The New York Times* that "there are factual mistakes, and then there are political mistakes"—and Biden's was the latter.

Biden's misadventures, which tended to strike when he ventured "off prompter," in his staff's anxious phrase, was part of the reason that political wags so often underestimated his potential. Many Americans outside of Washington greeted those moments with a shrug. In fact, Biden's off-the-cuff moments at Harvard distracted from what was, in retrospect, a prescient appraisal of foreign affairs, in which he drew connections between crises—ISIS, Ukraine, Ebola—and growing territorial tensions with authoritarian powers. Biden called for strengthening NATO, helping "small nations resist the blackmail and coercion of larger powers using new asymmetric weapons" (a reference to Russia and China). He described a new era defined by an "incredible diffusion of power within states and among states that has led to greater instability" requiring "a global response involving more players, more *diverse* players than ever before."

Over the years, I have come to recognize a few distinct sources of Biden's twilight war with his mouth. The most common is the Biden crime of passion. During the battle over implementation of the Affordable Care Act, in 2014, Biden was talking to reporters outside Butterfield's Pancake House, in Scottsdale, Arizona. He spotted a young woman on a bench and bounded over to enlist her as a prop, pitching her on the need to sign up for insurance under the Affordable Care Act: "Do it for your parents! Give them peace of mind!" he implored. She nodded gamely, but, after he had moved on, she conceded that she couldn't sign up because she was a tourist visiting from Canada. ("I just didn't know if I should say.") Other times, his comments detonated on arrival because he knew full well that they would. In a White House event on protecting students from sexual assault, Biden once said that, where he came from, when "a man raised his hand to a woman, you had the job to kick the living crap out of him if he did it. Excuse my language."

Part of the problem was that Biden learned his habits in Congress, where members do not receive the kind of constant attention that settles on a president or vice president. His words inhabited a no-man's-land between quality and quantity. Most of what he said went unrecorded, and so if he said something unfortunate, it was generally swept away in the ambient wind produced by his colleagues. Once he was tapped as a VP candidate, however, his statements were parsed. Biden accepted that scrutiny as the price of candor. He told me, "I don't say very much I don't really think through. I know that sounds inconsistent with Joe Biden."

In the usual telling, Joseph Robinette Biden Jr. is a product of the Silent Generation, the cohort of cautious Americans born between the Great Depression and the end of the Second World War, who were too young to have fought overseas and too old to lead the counterculture. The nickname was popularized by William Manchester, in 1959, who found them "withdrawn" and "unimaginative," but the image never sufficed to account for a generation that encompassed Muhammad Ali, Elvis Presley, and Ruth Bader Ginsburg.

More important was this: to be born in America in 1942 as a white heterosexual male was, generally speaking, to win a cosmic lottery. Because of low birth rates during the Depression and the war, the generation was exceptionally small—the first in American history to be smaller than the one before it. Its members enjoyed more attention and resources from their parents, smaller class sizes, and high rates of college admission. The New Deal and the G.I. Bill gave them benefits, loans, and federal work programs, which thrust millions of white Americans into the middle class. The sociologist Elwood Carlson, assessing their fortunes in his book *The Lucky Few*, described an age when American companies expanded workforces, built pensions, and distributed stock— a combination that produced "the financially luckiest generation of the twentieth century."

Their advantages shaped their ideas about government, money, race, and opportunity. In an essay for *Harper's*, a year after Biden was born, E. B. White had captured a particular breed of postwar American swagger: "The Society of Movers and Doers," he wrote, "is a very pompous society indeed, whose members solemnly accept all the responsibility for their own eminence and success." They were a homogeneous lot; nearly nine out of ten were white and born in the United States. They tended, as Carlson put it, to "view their successes in life as their own achievements, rather than thinking in terms of the social context that made their success possible." In politics, their right wing included "the most conservative Republicans of any generation in the twentieth century."

Biden fit the mold in some respects and defied it in others. The eldest of four siblings, he was ten when his father, out of a job, moved the family from Scranton, Pennsylvania, to Delaware. The father, known as "Big Joe," cleaned boilers and sold cars. Big Joe had been wealthy as a young man, but business soured; vestiges of his brush with prosperity were a polo mallet in the closet and an acute sensitivity to signs of disrespect. Once, at an office Christmas party, the boss tossed a bucket of silver dollars onto the dance floor and watched the salesmen scramble to pick them up. "Dad sat frozen for a second," his son wrote, in a 2007 memoir called *Promises to Keep*. Then "he stood up, took my mom's hand, and walked out of the party," losing his job in the process.

Biden's mother reinforced the hyper-alertness to status. "She told us, from the time we were little kids: Nobody is better than you," his sister, Valerie Biden Owens, said. "And you're no better than anybody else." The Bidens adhered to an old-neighborhood conception of loyalty. "It's the glue that holds society together," he told me. "If you weren't loyal, you were just not a worthy person." Biden liked to tell a story about his father getting duped by a business partner. When prosecutors asked him to testify, Big Joe said, "I can't. I'm godfather to his daughter."

When Biden reflects on his childhood, he lingers most

on the experience of having a stutter. "I talked like Morse code. Dot-dot-dot-dot-dash-dash-dash-dash," he wrote. "It was like having to stand in the corner with the dunce cap. Other kids looked at me like I was stupid. They laughed." He went on, "Even today I can remember the dread, the shame, the absolute rage, as vividly as the day it was happening." Reading Latin was hell. He told me, "I had only been in school three weeks, and I was nicknamed Joe Impedimenta, because I had an impediment. I couldn't speak."

When Biden tells it, the story of overcoming his "impedimenta" rests mostly on will and perseverance. As a practical matter, getting over his stutter required navigating the world with shortcuts. "You just learn to anticipate what you think you're going to be confronted with," he said, and offered an example: "I know he's gonna ask me about the Phillies game, or the Yankees game. So why don't I cauterize this at the outset, and say, 'How 'bout those Yankees?' Because you can practice, as you're walking up." He dropped his voice to a whisper: "How about those Yankees, how about those Yankees." He took to reciting passages—Yeats, Emerson, the Declaration of Independence—and by his sophomore year in high school the stutter was giving way.

He never entirely shed the insecurity. Over the years, I've heard him return over and over to matters of respect and vulnerability. He can still name the grade school students who humiliated him. And, in office, aides learned quickly that Biden was especially wary of embarrassment. A former adviser recalled prepping Biden to ask a European leader for a favor; when the leader unexpectedly said no, Biden froze: "He hangs up the phone, and he's like, 'Don't ever set me up like that again. It's okay if we can't move the ball; I'll still make the call, but you've got to tell me.'"

But through sheer will, he also honed the capacity to give a rousing speech. Importantly, and a bit ominously, he learned that keeping the attention of his crowd often required going off script. "If I felt myself losing them, I would extemporize, tell a joke, focus in on a single person who wasn't paying attention and call him out," he wrote. "I fell in love with the idea of being able to sway a jury—and being able to see it happen right before my eyes."

Unlike the greater Washington orators who inspired or surrounded him—John F. Kennedy, Daniel Patrick Moynihan, Bill Clinton, Obama—Biden's was not a gift; it was a product of labor. Steve Solarz, the late New York congressman, once visited the Senate at night and found the chamber nearly empty. "There was one person on the floor, orating as though it were the Roman Colosseum, and it was Joe Biden," he told a staffer. "This guy was just working it, like a tennis pro."

• • •

Biden was a middling but popular student at Archmere Academy, a private day school in Delaware; to defray his tuition, he worked on a grounds crew. He won a race for junior-class president and won again the next year. In his memoir, he resorted to the third-person to confess, "Joe Biden wasn't hitting the library on very many Saturday nights." That fed an intellectual insecurity that lingers and nudges him to grasp a bit too lustily at a statistic, or to plunge headlong into the classics. (After the Shylock moment, Foxman said, "Joe and I agreed that perhaps he needs to bone up on his Shakespeare.")

He went on to the University of Delaware, where he played football and worked one summer as a lifeguard at a public pool, where he came to know young Black men who lived in a nearby housing project. Brett Gadsden, a historian at Northwestern University who grew up near Wilmington and has written about its racial politics, describes the city as suspended between North and South—closer to New York City than to Raleigh, but still so segregated that African diplomats, driving through on the way to Washington, were sometimes denied service at rest stops. "There's probably a metaphorical lesson in the fact that Biden hails from a place that has this mythical reputation as a middle-ground state," Gadsden told me. "It's emblematic of a kind of imagined center."

Biden played bit parts in protests against segregation, including walking out of a Wilmington diner that refused to serve a Black classmate in 1961 and picketing the segregated Rialto movie theater the following year. Later, he sometimes exaggerated his role ("I marched"), but in 2013, during a ceremony commemorating the march in Selma, Biden expressed remorse that he had not done more. "I was involved in my state, in a small way, which was still fighting the lingering vestiges of Jim Crow," Biden told the audience, "but I regret and, although it's not part of what I'm supposed to say, apologize. It took me forty-eight years to get here. I should've been here."

In his junior year, he visited the Bahamas for spring break, where he met Neilia Hunter, an English major, and a daughter of diner owners in upstate New York. In the solemn prose of his memoir, "I fell ass over tin cup in love." He and Neilia married in 1966. He attended, barely, Syracuse University's law school, where he was, by his description, "a dangerous combination of arrogant and sloppy." He had to repeat a course because he was caught lifting five pages of a law review paper without footnoting but told administrators it was ignorance, not malice. ("I hadn't been to class enough to know how to do citations.")

He graduated seventy-sixth in a class of eighty-five, and moved to the suburbs of Wilmington, where he became a public defender. In 1972, after a short stint on the New Castle County Council, he made an audacious run for the U.S. Senate. He was an underdog, polling 30 points behind J. Caleb Boggs, a sixty-two-year-old veteran of World War II, who had held statewide office for twenty-five years. Biden, at twenty-nine, was so young that, on Election Day, he would still be constitutionally ineligible to take his seat. At events, people mistook him for the son of the Biden on the ballot, and reporters joked that he was not even as old as his opponent's shoes. Biden set out to turn the age problem into a political asset.

He played up his youth, campaigning with his photogenic family—wife Neilia, toddlers Beau and Hunter, and infant daughter Naomi—and publishing ads with the tagline "He understands what's happening today." The Wilmington *Evening Journal* observed that voters his age "get that 'new hero' look when Biden raps about how the old guard has bungled things." The family crisscrossed the state, attracting voters who opposed the war in Vietnam or were alienated from politics. Biden also developed an instinct for recognizing the outer limit to the criticism he could unleash without spoiling the mystique of his insurgency campaign. When Boggs struggled to come up with a fact during a debate, Biden resisted the urge to pounce, sensing, as he put it later, that "nobody in the audience wanted to see Boggs embarrassed—it would have been like clubbing the family's favorite uncle." By the time Boggs recognized the threat, it was too late to avoid one of the biggest upsets in Senate history. Biden won by just three thousand votes.

In the weeks before he was sworn in, he worked out of a borrowed office in Washington. His sister, Val, helped him get organized. On the afternoon of December 18, Biden's life came apart. His brother Jimmy called and asked to talk to Val. She turned white. "There's been a slight accident," she said. Biden sensed something in her voice; he felt it in his chest. "She's dead, isn't she?" he said.

Neilia had been at the wheel of their white Chevy station wagon, driving with the kids to get a Christmas tree, when a tractor-trailer, loaded with corncobs, hit them broadside, leaving the road littered with campaign brochures. Neilia and Naomi, the baby, were killed. Hunter, age two, suffered a head injury; Beau, who was three, was hospitalized for weeks with broken bones.

Biden, who until then had lived a life of almost preposterous good fortune, thought of suicide. In *What It*

Takes, the classic study of the minds of politicians, Richard Ben Cramer wrote of Biden's grief about the accident: "All of it, all of them—all they'd done—*did not matter*. Gone." The press wanted a simple tale of a stoic widower, Cramer wrote, but "Joe was so sick of it, he could puke."

He had been raised to believe in a benevolent God. "Well, I didn't want to hear anything about a merciful God. No words, no prayer, no sermon gave me ease. I felt God had played a horrible trick on me, and I was angry," he wrote later. He could not imagine taking his seat in the Senate, but party elders, such as Mike Mansfield, urged him to try Washington for six months. In the end, Biden took the seat, in part because he worried what would become of his sons if their father never recovered. He took the oath of office beside the hospital bed where Beau was lying in a cast.

"They had lost their mom and their sister, so they cannot lose their father, and that's what made him get out of bed in the morning," Val told me. She moved in and lived with her brother and the boys for four years. He never moved from Wilmington. As a single father, he began the ninety-minute commute each way on Amtrak, a daily ritual that put him outside of the Washington social scene, and would become a fixture of his life. Ted Kaufman, one of Biden's closest aides, told me, "Six months after the accident, he would come into the office and he would be in as bad a shape as he was the day of the accident. He had one of Neilia's rings, and he'd put it on his little finger. If he came into the office with that ring on his finger—oh, boy, you knew he was really hurting."

Over the years, Biden learned tactics for coping, a set of private strategies to tame his mind akin to the maneuvers he developed for overcoming his stutter. He kept a pen and pad beside his bed and rated each day from one to ten, to track his progress. He adopted his father's belief that fate eventually apportions each person, or each family, a balanced ledger of fortune. "The bigger the highs," he liked to say, "the deeper the troughs."

Later, he adopted a belief that had sustained Joseph P. Kennedy Sr., the Boston patriarch who buried four of his children. In a letter to a friend, Kennedy wrote, "When one of your loved ones goes out of your life, you think what he might have done with a few more years. . . . And you wonder what you are going to do with the rest of yours. Then one day, because there is a world to be lived in, you find yourself part of it, trying to accomplish something—something he did not have time enough to do. And perhaps that is the reason for it all."

CHAPTER 3

"Grow Up"

When Biden arrived in the Senate, in 1973, he focused mainly on staying there. A freshman profile in *Washingtonian* magazine noted, "Senator Biden doesn't believe issues make much difference in an election—personality and presentation are the key." He entered Congress just months after Richard Nixon had been reelected in a landslide, despite the growing investigation into the Watergate scandal.

In the early politics of his time in the Senate, Biden was careful to avoid becoming known as a liberal. National partisan polarization was at a historic low, and voters often divided their loyalties among candidates from multiple parties. In 1974, on the basis of his support of civil rights and opposition to the war in Vietnam, Biden received a high rating from Americans for Democratic Action, a progressive nonprofit group. He complained about it. "Those ADA ratings get us into so much trouble that a lot of us sit around thinking up ways to vote conservative," he told a reporter. "When it comes to civil rights and civil liberties, I'm a liberal, but that's it. I'm really quite conservative on most other issues. My wife said I was the most socially conservative man she had ever known."

At a community meeting that summer, white suburbanites heckled Biden for his willingness to support court-ordered busing. He became their champion—the Democratic Party's leading anti-busing crusader. Gadsden, of Northwestern, was among the students in the Wilmington area who were bused to a mostly Black school over Biden's opposition. "Personally, I think my classmates and I benefited greatly from the opportunity," he told me. "It is understandable, in a strict political sense, that Biden opposed busing in the early 1970s. As a matter of history, however, Biden purposefully chose to ignore a long record of violations against the constitutional rights of Black children." That put him "squarely within the liberal retreat from civil rights that dates back to the busing backlash and runs through President Clinton's politics of triangulation," he said.

In his early years, Biden faced constant snickers about his depth and gravitas. When Henry Kissinger was secretary of state, he mistook the boyish senator for a staffer; once alerted, Kissinger offered only a tepid correction: "I apologize, Senator Bidd-en," Kissinger said, mangling Biden's name. (Biden replied, with evident pique, "No problem, Secretary Dulles.") On the Senate floor, Biden once gave an impassioned speech on an unfamiliar subject—oil wells—and an opponent called him out. ("Senator Biden, have you ever *seen* a stripper well?") A former aide recalled, "He got his butt kicked. And from that day forward, he said 'I am always going to be completely prepared.'"

He pushed his staff to help him prepare answers to any conceivable question. He sought out scholars for information about unfamiliar topics. In May 1975, he wrote a letter to Hannah Arendt, the political theorist who explored the roots of authoritarianism:

> *Dear Miss Arendt,*
>
> *I read in a recent article by Tom Wicker of a paper that you read at the Boston Bicentennial Forum.*
>
> *As a member of the Foreign Relations Committee of the Senate, I am most interested in receiving a copy of your paper.*
>
> *Thank you.*
>
> *Sincerely,*
> *Joseph R. Biden Jr.*
> *United States Senator*

The paper to which Biden referred was "Home to Roost," a lecture Arendt read on May 20, 1975, at Boston's Faneuil Hall, one of her last public testaments before her death in December. In her paper, she warned, presciently, that the ascendant doctrines of the commercial world—the seemingly innocent deceptions of Madison Avenue, the business of puffery and public relations— were giving American politicians a greater power to deceive. Lying was as old as politics, she noted, but lying "as a way of life" was more common "in countries under totalitarian rule." She wrote: "When the facts come home to roost, let us try at least to make them welcome, let us not try to escape into some utopias—images, theories, or sheer follies. It was the greatness of this Republic to give due account to the best and the worst in man, all for the sake of Freedom."

As Biden rose in the Senate, he was rebuilding his family. Two and a half years after Neilia's death, his brother set him up on a blind date with Jill Jacobs, a senior studying English at the University of Delaware. She was an aspiring teacher from the Philadelphia suburbs. Jacobs puzzled over the man who was, as she put it, "nothing like the side-burned, bell-bottom-wearing guys I was used to dating." She'd worked part-time as a local model, and Biden recognized her from an ad at the airport. Jacobs did not want a life in politics, but she came to love Biden's sons.

In the Biden family, nothing was ever a solo decision. Two and a half years after Neilia's death, his sons asked, "Are we gonna get married again?" In 1977, after multiple proposals, she married him. They had a daughter, Ashley, who became a social worker.

In the decades that followed, Jill Biden retained as much of her life as possible; she became the first vice presidential spouse to continue working full-time, sharing a cubicle and teaching English at Northern Virginia Community College. When she and I sat down at a café near the White House, her security was unobtrusive, and nobody seemed to recognize her. In 2008, her husband had irritated some women voters by describing his wife as "drop-dead gorgeous." I asked what she'd made of that. "Sometimes I get a little put off by things he might say that are too personal for me," she said. "But, the thing is, I think Joe believes that." She laughed. "How can you get offended when your husband thinks that about you?"

By 1987, after fifteen years in the Senate, Biden was shedding some of the early doubts. As chairman of the Judiciary Committee, he was praised by Democrats for leading a successful battle against Robert Bork, Ronald Reagan's conservative nominee for the Supreme Court. That year, he made his first run for president, but in the spotlight his old insecurities and shortcuts bedeviled him. In his campaign stump speech, he had been quoting the British politician Neil Kinnock about rising from humble origins. But at the Iowa State Fair he didn't cite Kinnock—an unconscious mistake, he said—and absorbed the biography as his own, talking of "my ancestors who worked in the coal mines of northeast Pennsylvania and would come up after twelve hours."

There were no coal-mining ancestors. Reporters found another unattributed quote (from Robert Kennedy) and a tape of Biden with a crowd in New Hampshire, in which he overstated his academic record and boasted to a questioner, "I think I probably have a much higher I.Q. than you do!" Biden bragged that he'd received "a full academic scholarship" and "ended up in the top half of my class," neither of which was true. When he was asked about it, he apologized and said, "I exaggerate when I'm angry, but I've never gone around telling people things that aren't true about me." Around Capitol Hill, people joked, "The Kennedys quoted the Greeks; Biden quoted the Kennedys." He was getting a reputation as a pompous blowhard, and congressional staffers circulated a spoof résumé with Biden's picture and accomplishments, including "inventor of polyurethane and the weedeater" and "Member, Rockettes (1968)."

Biden's race was finished by the end of September; he had lasted less than four months. For years afterward, he still sometimes embellished his biography. He once said that he'd been "shot at" in Iraq. Pressed, he revised it to say, "I was near where a shot landed." Looking over the record of his exaggerations and plagiarism, I came to see them as the excesses of a man who wanted every story to sing, even at the risk of embarrassment. The costs of that weakness have been steep, but Biden only fitfully acknowledged them. When he announced his withdrawal from the presidential race in 1987, he conceded his mistakes but also cast blame on "the environment of presidential politics that makes it so difficult to let the American people measure the whole Joe Biden and not just misstatements that I have made." For years afterward, he blamed the loss on opposition research and an overzealous press. But, in 2007, Biden finally put aside the excuses about his failed presidential campaign. "The bottom line was, I made a mistake, and it was born out of my arrogance," he told a reporter. "I didn't deserve to be president."

Shortly after ending his presidential campaign, Biden suffered the aneurysm that left him on the floor of his hotel room. By Labor Day, he was back in Congress. In his public self-presentation, that marks the beginning of the resurrection. But a fuller accounting includes one more crucible: in 1991, Biden ran the hearings on Clarence Thomas's nomination to the Supreme Court. Biden enraged liberal supporters by not allowing the testimony of women who might have buttressed Anita

Hill's accusations of sexual harassment. Though Biden ultimately voted against him, Thomas won by a narrow margin, fifty-two to forty-eight. Biden, who omitted the Thomas hearings from his memoir, told Jane Mayer and Jill Abramson, for their book on the hearing, *Strange Justice*, that he had acted in "fairness to Thomas, which in retrospect he didn't deserve."

Biden worked hard to rebuild his reputation. In 1994 he led the effort to pass the Violence Against Women Act, which heightened protections against abusive partners, and helped him win back the support of women's groups. Biden loved the old cloak-room deal-making, the bipartisan courtesies, when people traded issues to arrive at some level of agreement. His alliances were so varied that he was the only senator who was asked to speak at funerals for Strom Thurmond, the former segregationist, John McCain, the Arizona Republican, and Frank Lautenberg, the Democratic senator from New Jersey, who called Biden "the only Catholic Jew." He told me, "You'd ask them for something in the political realm, they'd say, 'Okay.' And even if, by the time it came to do what had to be done, their circumstances had changed, they'd still do it."

He mourned the arrival of more combative members who "really had no respect for the institution of the Senate," he told me. "By that, I mean they wanted to make it the House. I'll never forget the first time I heard someone

on the floor of the Senate"—during the Clinton years—
"refer to the president as Bubba." Lawmakers were not just
abandoning some decorous courtesies; they were putting
their private political calculations above public interest.
"Today, it's a moving set of what a commitment is," Biden
said, and he did a pantomime of a mercenary member of
Congress. "'I know what I told you *then*, but *now*, God,
now I got a problem, so I can't be with you anymore.'"

In the Senate, Biden accrued a record that, to today's
progressives, resembles the counts in an indictment. He
voted for the deregulation of Wall Street, the Defense
of Marriage Act, the North American Free Trade Agreement, the war in Iraq. During the 2020 primaries, Massa-
chusetts senator Elizabeth Warren faulted him for having
legislated "on the side of the credit card companies." In a
headline, *Jacobin*, the socialist magazine, likened him to
a hapless movie character with a recurring role in pivotal
events of the twentieth century, calling him "the Forrest
Gump of the Democratic Party's Rightward Turn."

Nothing in Biden's record has dogged him more than
his role in drafting the 1994 crime bill, the most sweeping legislation of its kind in American history. The bill
contributed to the problems of mass incarceration by
creating a federal "three strikes" law, encouraging lon-

ger jail terms, and granting billions of dollars to states to build more prisons.

At the time, the bill had support from some Democrats on the left, including Bernie Sanders—"I'm not happy I voted for a terrible bill," he says now—and from Black political leaders, including Representative James E. Clyburn, of South Carolina. Clyburn had learned through difficult experience that many of his Black constituents were less enthusiastic than white liberals about criminal justice reform. At a town hall meeting in 1994, he had voiced skepticism about an initiative for stricter sentences. "I got my head handed to me in that meeting, and everybody in that meeting was Black," Clyburn told me recently. "Crack cocaine was a scourge in the Black communities. They wanted it out of those communities, and they had gotten very tough on drugs. And that's why yours truly, and other members of the Congressional Black Caucus, voted for that 1994 crime bill." Clyburn, like Biden, remains proud that the bill included the Violence Against Women Act, a ban on assault weapons, and money for community policing and drug courts. But, in the fall of 1994, Republicans took control of the House; Clyburn faults them for changes they instituted. "They kept all the punitive stuff and got rid of the good stuff," he said. Biden has offered similarly qualified regrets. "I know we haven't always gotten things right, but I've always tried," he said last year. "We thought we were told by the experts that crack, you never go back—that it was somehow fundamentally different. It's not different. But it has trapped an entire generation."

In *Locking Up Our Own*, a Pulitzer Prize–winning study of criminal justice and racial politics, James Forman Jr. describes mass incarceration as the consequence of "a series of small decisions, made over time, by a disparate group of actors." At bottom, they could be traced to what Forman calls the "politics of responsibility," a theory of personal discipline, consonant with the individualism of the Silent Generation and the boomers, that was voiced regularly at the top of the Democratic Party. In Bill Clinton's Inaugural Address in 1993, he vowed to "offer more opportunity to all and demand more responsibility from all."

It was a language inspired by the Republican playbook. In the late 1980s, after Democrats lost five out of six of the previous presidential contests, Clinton and others in the rising generation of Democrats had embraced the rhetoric of personal responsibility, which sought to draw clearer distinctions between those who were deemed to be deserving of benefits and those who were not. Ronald Reagan had declared, "We will never abandon those who, through no fault of their own, must have our help." The expression "through no fault of their own" had first appeared in presidential rhetoric under the conservatives Calvin Coolidge and Herbert Hoover, but Reagan used it more often than any prior president. Then, Clinton used it at least twice as many times as Reagan, according to a count by Michael Sandel, a Harvard political philosopher. In 1995, when Eric Holder was the first Black person to be U.S attorney for the District of Columbia, he launched Operation Ceasefire, which encouraged Washington police to stop cars and search for guns—a forerunner to the stop-and-frisk policy he later condemned as attorney general, under Obama. "I'm not going to be naive about it," Holder said at a community meeting in 1995. "The people who will be stopped will be young Black males, overwhelmingly."

Reflecting on the decisions of those years, Clyburn and his peers were not "trying to put people in jail," he said. "We were trying to respond to our communities' wishes." In addition to the crime bill, the politics of responsibility inspired welfare reform in 1996, which limited federal benefits for the poor, and bankruptcy legislation, supported by Biden, which made it harder for Americans to resolve their debts.

The emphasis on responsibility and accountability had a very different effect for people at the top. Clinton had campaigned on a promise to rein in the pay of CEOs, by capping a company's ability to deduct executive compensation from its taxes. But, in a bill that passed Congress after the election, Clinton's advisers added a loophole that exempted "performance" pay, such as stock options and bonuses, from the cap. As a result, CEO pay soared, because companies delivered ever larger sums for "performance." Biden came to rue his vote in favor of it. "It sounded right at the time, but what it did was, the market induces a response, and the response was, 'Okay, let's buy back our own stock, raise the value of that stock, and pay me in stock.'" (In the years immediately after the financial crash of 2007–2008, top executives at the twenty leading American banks received nearly $800 million in stock-based performance pay.)

When I asked Cornell William Brooks, the Harvard professor and former head of the NAACP, to assess Biden's record in Washington, he offered an image reminiscent of Biden's mental ledger of highs and lows. "People love the fact that he faithfully and well served the nation's first African American president—and hate his leadership on the crime bill. They are troubled by his positions on busing, but they measure him as a historical whole, and by the stature of his sincerity," Brooks said. "The things which are most disquieting about Joe Biden, to the progressive wing of the Democratic base, are the very things that are most disquieting about the Democratic Party."

• • •

He had an appetite for politics that was inexhaustible even by Washington standards. George Mitchell, the Democratic senator from Maine who came to serve as majority leader, resented that many of his colleagues had little interest in the unglamorous work of rallying votes behind the scenes. "Usually a senator would come to me, the majority leader, and say 'Well, here's a problem. Can you get the votes?' Then they'd go off to dinner." Biden was different; Mitchell recalled asking him to help call every Democratic senator at home, and then returned to check on him after several hours of calls. "I was up to No. 8, and he was still on No. 2," Mitchell said. "I said, 'Joe, I know you want to explain this thing to these guys, but you've to got be a little more concise.'"

In 2007, Biden ran for president a second time. He did well in debates—asked if he had "the discipline not to talk too much," he replied "yes" and fell silent. But he raised hardly any money and dropped out early. It looked like his run might be remembered for little more than a botched compliment to Obama, a fellow candidate, whom Biden described as "articulate and bright and clean and a nice-looking guy." When Biden was criticized for it, Obama defended him, saying, "I have absolutely no doubt about what is in his heart and the commitment that he has made with respect to racial equality in this country."

In fact, Biden's candidacy had impressed Obama, who began to call him for advice on national security and foreign policy. Before a committee hearing, Biden helped Obama prepare for the questioning of General David Petraeus, after which Obama was applauded for his performance. Obama also came to admire the depth of Biden's relationships abroad. Mitchell remembers welcoming visiting heads of state to Capitol Hill. "I'd say, 'Here's Senator Smith, here's Senator Jones.' When I got to Joe, the leader would look out and say, 'Hi, Joe.'" As in domestic politics Biden took a broad view of potential partners in foreign affairs. "You can drop him into Kazakhstan or Bahrain, it doesn't matter—he's gonna find some Joe Blow that he met thirty years ago who's now running the place," Julianne Smith, his former deputy national security advisor, told me. "And it doesn't even matter what the political stripes are: he knows conservatives, he knows social democrats, because, over thirty-five-plus years, everybody came to the Senate Foreign Relations Committee."

After Obama secured the nomination, he called Biden to ask if he would allow himself to be vetted for vice presidential consideration. Biden declined, asking his aides, Can anyone even *name* Lincoln's vice president? But Jill

Biden urged him to reconsider. She told me, "I was angry at George Bush for getting us into that war. To me, it was so senseless." She had pushed her husband to run for president, because, she said, "You've got to end that war." Now the vice presidency was another chance. Moreover, she added, "Joe started out in politics because of civil rights. And then for this to evolve and then come to this historic moment, with the first Black man ever elected to be president of the United States, and for Joe to be a major part of that, I thought was really almost a fairy tale."

There was only one problem. "What was it going to be like to be No. 2?" she said. "And for him to be supporting someone else's positions?" Biden had never worked for anyone, and he was not sure he could. He told a friend about the decisive conversation with his wife. He asked her, "How am I going to handle this?" To which she replied, "Grow up."

CHAPTER 4

Veep

Presidential tickets are often shotgun marriages, and Biden and Obama were an especially dissimilar pair. By politicians' standards, Obama projected feline indifference to the adoration he engendered. Biden reached for every hand, shoulder, and head. They were separated by nineteen years and a canyon in style. Obama was a technocrat, Biden the gut politician. Obama was the peripatetic mixed-race son of Hawaii, Indonesia, Kenya, and Chicago, a child of the 1970s who experimented with "a little blow." Biden had grown up with two parents, three siblings, and a Sunday routine: "Dad would give me a dollar, and I'd pedal off to Cutler's Pharmacy to fetch a half-gallon of Breyers ice cream. I'd ride back and we'd all six sit around the living room to watch *Lassie* and *Jack Benny* and *Ed Sullivan*."

When Obama recruited Biden to join the ticket, some Democrats were baffled. The Obama presidency was supposed to mark a new chapter in the generational story of American politics, the triumph of what Stacey Abrams, the voting rights activist and former Georgia gubernatorial candidate, later called the "new American majority"—a coalition of "people of color, young people, and moderate to progressive whites." Biden had failed to crack one percent in the Iowa caucuses. But Obama admired his feisty debate performance, his knowledge of foreign leaders, and his connections in D.C. Biden was also, as David Axelrod, Obama's chief strategist, put it to me, "culturally and geographically well situated": he made Obama more attractive to older working-class Midwestern whites, who might not feel a natural connection to a Black former community organizer.

Axelrod also sensed that Biden had a strength that was hard to convey in the usual language of politics. During the vetting process, he had visited Biden at home in Delaware and watched his dealings with his family. "He was talking to Beau and said, 'I'll be by later to see the kids,'" Axelrod recalled. "I have a recollection that he kissed him. He said, 'I love you.'" When Axelrod got back to Washington, he told Obama, "There's something really special about this family." In Washington, family is often wielded as a prop. But this was something different. "It's not a thing; it's real," Axelrod told Obama. "I don't know how that plays into all this, but it seems to me to be a real asset."

They had to get to know each other. Biden was irritated by some of Obama's young staff, and Obama aides worried about Biden's unplanned utterances. The vice president was unaccustomed to teleprompters. Because of his stutter, reading aloud was still more awkward for him than extemporizing. Sometimes he worked with speechwriters and then ignored the script, which left him vulnerable to what members of Obama's campaign team called Joe Bombs, the things he says but doesn't mean ("Folks, I can tell you I've known eight presidents, three of them intimately") and the things he means but shouldn't say.

At a campaign stop in South Philadelphia, Ed Rendell, the governor of Pennsylvania at the time, was surprised to find workers erecting a teleprompter for Biden. "I said, 'Why does Joe have a teleprompter? He never uses a teleprompter.' And they said to me, on the QT, sort of, 'Well, the Obama campaign wants him to be totally scripted, so he doesn't make any mistakes.'" In February 2009, after the Inauguration, Biden told an audience that there was a "30 percent chance we're going to get it wrong" on the economy. A reporter asked the president about it, and Obama said, "I don't remember exactly what Joe was referring to. Not surprisingly."

Over lunch at the White House, Biden raised the PR problem, saying that a divide would harm both of them. Obama agreed; he promised to watch his words. "The vice president asked for one thing," Rahm Emanuel, Obama's first chief of staff, recalled. "That he could always comment, would never be shut down, and he'd be the last guy in the room to talk to him. And the president lived up to that commitment." Likewise, Biden said, "The deal the president asked for was that we would each commit that, when anything was on our minds, when something the other was doing was bothering us, we'd say so."

In Delaware, a state with half as many people as the city of Houston, Biden had been the most famous politician for more than four decades. Bumper stickers for his Senate campaigns said simply, "JOE." But, once he was in the White House, Biden had to find a role with purpose and productivity. Until recently, vice presidents were a long way from power. Daniel Webster declined the job in 1848, saying, "I do not propose to be buried until I am really dead and in my coffin." While Coolidge held the job, he prided himself on getting eleven hours of sleep each night. But in the decades after the Second World War, as the speed and the range of White House decisions grew, vice presidential power rose. With no fixed job description, each incumbent took his own approach: Al Gore pursued niche projects (the environment, Reinventing Government), and Dick Cheney guarded what an aide called the "iron issues" (defense, energy).

At first, Biden expected to be a vice president along the

lines of Lyndon Johnson, who had a similarly long tenure in Congress and served a younger president. Later, after reading *The Passage of Power*, the fourth volume of Robert Caro's biography of Johnson, Biden realized just how frustrated Johnson had been: "His opinion wasn't asked on anything, from the Bay of Pigs to the Cuban missile crisis. He just wasn't in the deal." In Joe Biden's political vocabulary, nothing was more important than being "in the deal." Instead of the Johnson model, he tried to emulate Walter Mondale. Under Jimmy Carter, Mondale had rejected small-bore assignments and moved his office from the Eisenhower Executive Office Building to the West Wing. "My job was to be a general adviser to the president," Mondale told me. Mondale, like Biden, had spent more than three decades in Congress, and tried to be a link between it and a president who lacked those connections. "Obama was green. He had been around the federal government only a short while," Mondale said. "He'd been, of course, very successful. But he was not seasoned in these things. Joe was. It fit a hole that had to be filled."

When Biden signed on to be vice president, his only requirement was a guarantee that he would be "in the deal"—in every meeting that mattered, never unable to reach the president, worthy of inclusion. Obama agreed, adding, "I want your point of view, Joe. I just want it in ten-minute increments, not sixty-minute increments."

• • •

Biden's office in the West Wing, seventeen steps from the Oval Office, was decorated like a classic hotel: dark wood, heavy drapes, walls and carpet in navy blue. There were portraits of John Adams and Thomas Jefferson, the first two occupants of the vice presidency. (Adams complained that the job was "the most insignificant office that ever the invention of man contrived.") But Biden took a more nuanced view. "It's all what the president makes it," he told me one day, during an interview over lunch in his office. Biden had come to the job half suspecting that he could do things better than a young, inexperienced president, but after six months he was humbled by Obama's command of a complex financial crisis that offered few political dividends. "I believe Barack Obama's leadership averted a long, drawn-out depression," Biden told me, adding, "The hardest action to take as a leader, as a parent, as a politician, as a priest, whatever it is, is the one that prevents the bad thing," because you can never prove that you prevented something worse.

Every morning, Biden walked down the hall to sit beside the president in the Oval Office, for briefings on intelligence and the economy. He had an open invitation to join the president's regular sessions with the secretaries of state and defense. As a senator, Biden had been critical of Cheney's accumulation of power, but, once in the White House, he held on to some of Cheney's innovations. Before Cheney, vice presidents did not routinely attend the Principals Committee, which consists of the president's top national security aides. Cheney almost always attended. Biden did so about a third of the time.

Obama developed enough confidence in Biden to assign him some of their most sensitive tasks. When the White House needed to pass the $787 billion stimulus plan, Emanuel asked Biden to call six Republican senators. He got yes votes from three of them, and the bill passed by three votes. Biden coached Sonia Sotomayor before her Supreme Court confirmation hearings and led a lobbying effort to lure Senator Arlen Specter, a Pennsylvania Republican, to change parties. Also Biden helped nail down votes for the Affordable Care Act, the most ambitious social legislation since Lyndon Johnson's Great Society.

Obama asked him to oversee the spending of the economic stimulus funds, managing a vast array of local and state interests. Biden joked that he was the only member of the administration who couldn't be fired, and he aimed to be candid in internal White House debates. "Every president would say the hardest commodity to come by in the Oval Office is the truth and nothing but the truth, no matter how much it hurts," Bruce Reed, who was Biden's chief of staff from 2011 to 2013, said. "It's not always appreciated at the time, but it's the role everyone around a president should aspire to."

On policy, they had disagreements. In 2011, Biden objected to an administration plan to require Catholic hospitals and other institutions to cover contraceptives under the Affordable Care Act, saying that it would cost them working-class votes. Some of Obama's political advisers concluded that Biden's political radar was out of date. But, beneath the policy differences, Biden and Obama shared a basic belief that Americans craved unity in politics. Running for president, Obama called attention to fraying social bonds. He told an audience in 2008, "I'm talking about an empathy deficit, the inability to recognize ourselves in one another, to understand that we are our brother's keeper and our sister's keeper— and, in the words of Dr. King, we are all tied together in a 'single garment of destiny.'"

Biden's vision was less transcendent. "Look," he told me, "I never expect a foreign leader I'm dealing with, or a colleague senator, a congressperson, to voluntarily appear in the second edition of *Profiles in Courage*. So, you got to think of what is in their interest." And yet Biden's accounting of political interests sometimes nudged him closer to progressives. In May 2012, while Obama was weighing an endorsement of same-sex marriage, Biden beat him to it, telling an interviewer that he was "absolutely comfortable" with married gays and lesbians having full legal rights. Obama forgave him, but the president's political advisers were apoplectic. Biden staffers heard that his public activities were going to be curtailed for the week. Many outsiders saw the moment as a typical Biden gaffe, but White House officials recognized a pattern in Biden's calculations. "He is very much a weathervane for what the center of the left is," a senior Obama administration official told me. "He can see, 'Okay, this is where the society is moving. This is where the Democratic Party is moving, so I'm going to move.'"

Biden became an envoy to an implacable Congress, tapping the relationships he had built over the decades. David Plouffe, one of Obama's political advisers, saw Biden's mission as a question: "Where is the deal space?" His belief in compromise over ideology put him closer to the president. "They really have the same mind-set there," Plouffe said. Biden held on to his locker at the Senate gym, where he liked to kibbitz. "He just gathers intelligence," a former aide recalled. "He'll call one leader, then he'll call the leader of the other party, then he'll call five members who are just friends who level with him about what's going on."

At times, though, Democrats grew irritated by Biden's belief that he should manage Republican leaders toward compromise. In the last days of 2012, Bush-era tax cuts were set to expire, which would have raised $3.7 trillion in revenue over the next decade. To try to keep the tax cuts, Republicans threatened to default on the U.S. debt for the first time in history. Biden negotiated a last-minute compromise with McConnell, the Senate minority leader: they agreed to recoup $600 billion of that revenue, while allowing some tax cuts to become permanent. Harry Reid, the Senate majority leader, was said to be so appalled by the terms that he threw the paperwork in a fireplace. (Reid denied that.)

On a sunny weekend morning in 2014, five years after he had taken on the job of vice president, Biden was standing near the locker rooms at the University of Delaware's Tubby Raymond Field, preparing to give the commencement address. Each of the VIPs was wearing an academic robe and a flouncy velvet cap, except Biden, who skipped the headgear. (Biden rule No. 1: No funny hats. Biden rule No. 2: Don't change your brand.) An organizer guided him to a piece of masking tape on the floor, marked "vpotus," and they marched out to a cheering crowd of four thousand graduates in royal blue robes. When the provost made the introduction, he got carried away and called Biden "the forty-seventh President of the United States!" The crowd half laughed, half gasped, but nobody, including Biden, corrected him. After the speech, just before Biden ducked back inside, a young man cupped his hands and yelled, "Stay gangster, Joe! I dig you, man." Biden looked up, pleased but perplexed by an image he didn't control or entirely recognize. He waved and kept walking.

Over the years, Biden had acquired a singular place in the pop culture of American politics. In a White House that privileged self-containment, Biden ambled between exuberant and self-defeating. Instead of raging against the indignities of the vice presidency, Biden luxuriated in the job. Perched in his chair during the State of the Union address, peering down on his former congressional colleagues, Biden made a pistol out of his finger and thumb, and blasted away, winking and gunning with no evident irony. In 2013, C-SPAN taped him getting ready to swear in new senators. He greeted each senator's family with frisky enthusiasm. To the old ladies, he'd say, "You've got beautiful eyes, Mom, holy mackerel." To the young women: "Remember—no serious guys till you're thirty!" To the little kids in their Sunday best: "Take care of your grandfather. Your most important job." The full package—the Ray-Ban aviators, the shameless schmaltz, the echoes of the Fonz—never endeared him to the establishment, but it lent him an air of authenticity that was rare in his profession. It has also produced a whiff of cult appeal, such that his image came to have more in common with Betty White than with John Boehner, the long-serving Ohio congressman who was Speaker of the House at the time. In May 2014, after a teenager invited Biden to her prom, he replied with a corsage and a handwritten note encouraging her to "enjoy your prom as much as I did mine." On Twitter, people went fondly berserk.

Biden had an inexhaustible appetite for "the connect"—the rope line, the hand cupped around the back of the head, the eye contact with a skeptic in the crowd. "He kind of brings them in and hugs them, verbally, and sometimes physically," John Kerry, who was secretary of state at the time, told me. "He's a very tactile politician, and it's all real. None of it's put on." At a reception following a televised debate in 2008, John Marttila, a political adviser, thought he would help Biden make an exit. "I was repeatedly standing up and saying, 'Well, I think it's time to head off.' And he stayed there. I think we went to bed at two o'clock, and the wake-up call was five or five-thirty." To a degree that is rare among politicians, Marttila said, "the process of meeting people energizes him." Biden is such a close talker that he occasionally bumps his forehead into you mid-chat, a gesture so minor that it's notable only when you try to picture Barack Obama doing the same thing.

But Biden has always resented what he called the Uncle Joe Syndrome—the image of a dopey, undisciplined good ol' boy. The White House Correspondents' Association dinner, the annual gala put on by the press corps, once featured a video skit based on *Veep*, the HBO comedy starring Julia Louis-Dreyfus as a desperately ambitious vice president. When the series debuted, in 2012, Biden had given it a wide berth. ("Had I been working for his administration, I would've told him the same," Louis-Dreyfus told me.) But he had warmed to the show, and, for the correspondents' dinner, Biden appeared with Louis-Dreyfus in a skit in which the two Veeps run amok: they get tattoos with Nancy Pelosi, they break into the *Washington Post* offices to rewrite headlines, including "BIDEN IS RIDIN' HIGH: APPROVAL RATINGS OF 200%." Reviews of the evening declared the video a success, even if David Weigel, who covered politics for *Slate* at the time, observed that the jokes at Biden's expense contained a subtle hint that "the White House was gently, gingerly embracing the truth that Biden won't be his party's nominee for president" in 2016. A couple of days after the correspondents' dinner, I asked Biden what he thought of the skit. He said, "It actually turned out to be kind of funny," but added that he had tailored the script to avoid undue silliness. He said that a scene in which he and Louis-Dreyfus were caught eating ice cream in the

White House kitchen called for him to cower in front of Michelle Obama. "The first lady comes and I'm going to cower? That doesn't fit type," Biden said.

Outside the White House, Biden attracted widely divergent public appraisals. In a column before the 2012 election, Bill Keller, the former executive editor of *The New York Times*, urged Obama to drop Biden as a running mate and replace him with the secretary of state at the time, Hillary Clinton. (The campaign studied the idea, too, until polls showed that it would make no difference.) That March, declassified documents seized in the raid that killed Osama bin Laden included an unexpected insult: bin Laden had advised assassins to spare Biden and target Obama, telling them, "Biden is totally unprepared for that post, which will lead the U.S. into a crisis." That summer, a survey by the Pew Research Center and *The Washington Post* asked people to come up with a single word to describe Biden; the most frequent responses, nearly equal in number, were "good" and "idiot." Republicans rejoiced in casting Biden as the consummate pol, careless, blustery, and a fogy. "Vice President Joe Biden's in town," Senator Ted Cruz said, at a dinner for South Carolina conservatives at the time. "You know the great thing is you don't even need a punch line? You just say that and people laugh."

And, yet, in the final month of the 2012 campaign,

Biden reminded everyone why he was on the ticket. After Obama delivered a disastrously muted performance in a debate against Mitt Romney, the vice president prepared to face his counterpart, Paul Ryan, the then forty-two-year-old Wisconsin congressman, who had the eyes of a foal. Onstage, Biden wore a lupine grin. He guffawed, taunted, and interrupted. (When Ryan said, "Jack Kennedy lowered tax rates and created growth," Biden cut him off: "Oh, now you're Jack Kennedy!") The theatrics drove some viewers crazy, but the campaign was thrilled; Biden had arrested the slide, and when Obama prepared for his next debate advisers reportedly told him to channel some of Biden's pugnacious energy. By the end of 2012, the White House was extending him the ritual courtesy of hailing the power of its No. 2. A headline in *The Atlantic* asked, "The Most Influential Vice President in History?"

Above all, like much in Biden's life, his relationship to Obama was built on loyalty. Once you become vice president, Biden said, "you have an obligation to back up whatever he does, unless you have a fundamental moral dilemma with what he's doing." He added, "If I ever got to that point, I'd announce I had prostate cancer and I had to leave." At a Democratic Caucus lunch, after the party had lost the House of Representatives, the then congressman Anthony Weiner criticized Obama for making a deal with Republicans on tax cuts. Biden erupted, saying, "There's no goddamn way I'm going to stand here and talk about the president like that." A short while later, he unleashed a similar blast at Israeli prime minister Benjamin Netanyahu, who had found fault with elements of Obama's Middle East policy. When the president was criticized, Biden "muscled up," Plouffe said. The stories reached Obama. Ben Rhodes, who was the deputy national security advisor for strategic communications, told me at the time, "He knows the vice president has his back." The more flak Obama absorbed in Washington, the more he came to value Biden's defenses. "I think the battles built up a degree of trust that is now implicit in their relationship," Rhodes said.

They were both prideful men, and they had not expected to learn from each other, but, over time, the effect of their relationship was visible to those around them. Leon Panetta, who headed the CIA and, later, the Pentagon, for Obama, told me that Obama recognized a gap in his experience and his skills. "He is, deep down, a law professor, and I think there's a certain amount of 'Do I really have to do this?' kind of thing. And Joe represents that shadow that can say to the president of the United States, 'Yes, you got to do it.'" Obama took to saying to aides and audiences that naming Biden vice president was the best political decision he had made. "I think

Biden gets a lot of lessons from Obama's discipline, and that's instructive at times, even though it annoys him," a former Biden aide said. "And I think Obama learns from Joe's warmth. When they're in a meeting together, the foreigners will tilt toward Biden more than Obama." The aide added, "Each one feels like he is the mentor." When Biden entered the job, he had told David Axelrod, he still thought "I'd be the best president." But, after a year of observing Obama, Biden told Axelrod that he had been mistaken: "The right guy won, and I'm just really proud to be associated with him."

The trials facing the president and the vice president had brought them closer than many expected—not least of all themselves. Biden adviser John Marttila told me, "Joe and Barack were having lunch, and Obama said to Biden, 'You and I are becoming good friends! I find that very surprising.' And Joe says, '*You're* fucking surprised!'"

They were past their early awkwardness around Biden's ungovernable mouth, and Obama's weakness for condescension. But the tensions were not gone entirely, and they would come roaring back with implications not only for the 2016 election, but for 2020 as well.

CHAPTER 5

Envoy

O f all the jobs that fell to Biden in the White House, none consumed more of his energy than foreign affairs. Obama had scarce experience in it when he came to office, and Biden had been chairman of the Senate Committee on Foreign Relations. In Biden's diplomatic phrasing, the president "sends me to places that he doesn't want to go."

On Easter Sunday 2014, he boarded Air Force Two, bound for Kiev, the Ukrainian capital that had been descending, for months, into a chaotic standoff with Russia. It had begun the previous winter, when Ukraine's president Viktor Yanukovych sided with Moscow by scrapping an agreement with the European Union, triggering protests across the country. As with many foreign leaders, Biden had known Yanukovych for years, and maintained a towel-snapping rapport. "He was gregarious," Biden recalled. "I said, 'You look like a thug!' I said,

'You're so damn big.' " As the protests escalated, Biden tried to persuade Yanukovych to reconcile with the demonstrators. They spoke by phone nine times. But Biden's efforts failed. On February 20 the government's snipers opened fire on protesters, killing at least eighty-eight people in forty-eight hours. The president fled, leaving his subjects to pry open his mansion and find the fruits of his kleptocracy: pet peacocks, a fleet of antique cars, a private restaurant in the shape of a pirate ship. In the aftermath, Russian forces swept into Crimea, and Vladimir Putin christened it Russian soil.

Two months had passed since Yanukovych's flight, and Biden's mission on this trip was short and specific: the arrival of America's second-highest-ranking official was intended to reassure Ukraine's fragile government, and deter Putin from moving deeper into Ukrainian territory. Compared with the commander in chief, the vice president flies in remarkably restrained splendor. The modified Boeing 757 was well used. An armrest came off in a passenger's hands. The vice president had a private cabin with a foldout bed, a desk, and a guest chair, but if a second visitor arrived a plastic cooler passed as a seat. "If you want the trappings, it's a hell of a lot better to go into some other line of work," Biden said.

Air Force Two touched down in Kiev, a city with gracious boulevards, chestnut trees, and so many domed churches that the Bolsheviks declared it unfit to be a communist capital. The fighting in the city was finished, but the encampment at the Maidan, the city's main square, which had been the center of protests, still resembled a set for *Les Misérables*: tall, jagged barricades of metal, timber, and tires marked the battle lines. Sparks rose from open-air fires. In one of the few signs of recovery, the cobblestones that had been pried up to hurl at the police were stacked and ready for repaving.

At the parliament, a Stalin-era building with a colonnaded entrance, Biden was ushered in to see a group of politicians who were vying to lead the new government. After so many years, he has an arsenal of opening lines that he can deploy in Baghdad, Beijing, or Wilmington. One of his favorites: "If I had hair like yours, I'd be president." He often adapts his routine to fit the circumstances. In Kiev, he approached Vitali Klitschko, a six-foot-seven former heavyweight boxing champion who was known as Dr. Ironfist before he entered politics. Biden peered up and gave a hammy clench to Klitschko's right biceps. Moving down the table, he met Petro Poroshenko, a presidential candidate and billionaire who had made his fortune in the candy business. Biden, who was already considering a run for the presidency in 2016, told the group, "I've twice been a presidential candidate and I hope you do better than I did." (The next month, Poroshenko won the presidency.)

Biden took his seat at the head of the table. For his hosts in Kiev, the vice president had only a small aid package to announce: $58 million in election help, energy expertise, and nonlethal security equipment, including radios for the border patrol. More important, Biden wanted to convey a message to the new leaders in Kiev that regaining legitimacy would require changes beyond just resisting Russian interference. On a corruption index produced by Transparency International, Ukraine was ranked No. 144, tied with the Central African Republic, out of 177 countries. Biden told those seated around him, "To be very blunt about it, and this is a delicate thing to say to a group of leaders in their house of parliament, but you have to fight the cancer of corruption that is endemic in your system right now." Biden favors candor in such settings. In 1979, on one of his first trips to the Soviet Union, he listened to an argument from his Soviet counterpart, and replied, "Where I come from, we have a saying: You can't shit a shitter." Bill Bradley, a fellow senator on the delegation, later asked the American interpreter how he had translated Biden's comment into Russian. "Not literally," the interpreter said.

In his approach to foreign affairs, Biden sometimes irritates career diplomats. "They'll give me a line and I'll say,

'I'm not gonna say that! That's simply not believable!'" he told me. "You've got to start off with the assumption: the other guy's not an idiot. And most people aren't stupid about their own naked self-interest." Biden prided himself on being able to read people. He told me, "It's really very important, if you are able, to communicate to the other guy that you understand his problem. And some of this diplomatic bullshit communicates 'We have no idea of your problem.'"

Leon Panetta recalled listening to Biden work the phone at the White House: "You didn't know whether he was talking to a world leader or the head of the political party in Delaware." On overseas trips, Biden looked for chances to project a down-to-earth face of American power. In 2011, when I was living in China, Biden prepared to make an official visit to Beijing. At the time, the Communist Party was weathering a string of embarrassing illustrations of official privilege. In a prominent case, a bus carrying a mayor in Hebei province had run a red light and hit a fourteen-year-old student. The student was left disabled; the mayor never visited the hospital, which critics took as a sign of pompous seclusion. Even before Biden arrived in China, liberal young Chinese commentators on social media were enlisting him as a counterexample. Praising him for an ability to laugh at himself, they pointed to a video clip from the White

House Correspondents' Association dinner, in which Joe Wong, a Chinese-American comedian, told the crowd he'd read Biden's memoir and then met him in person. "I think the book is much better," Wong deadpanned, and the camera cut to Biden, in black tie nearby, howling with laughter.

In Beijing, Biden drove home the point; during a lunch break in the official meetings, he ventured out of the sterile confines that usually entrap official guests, and headed for a working-class canteen called Yao Ji Stewed Liver. The restaurant specializes in a soup, as a local reviewer put it, that is "dark and thick, filled with chunks of gritty liver and circles of soft but resistant intestines." Biden and his entourage squeezed in among the patrons, and the owner came out to shake his hand. To the startled diners, Biden apologized: "You came in for a quiet lunch, and I show up." Liberal Chinese commentators loved the scene, and, for years afterward, the restaurant carried a "Biden special" on the menu.

Other countries came to expect a certain unguided candor from him. When he was readying a visit to Tokyo in 2013, *The Asahi Shimbun*, a Japanese newspaper, prepared its readers. "He may be having the time of his life, but many around him fear he might get carried away and say something outrageous," an editorial explained. "Biden is known to have made slips of the tongue, but that apparently is also what makes him affable and interesting."

The full Biden played better around the Mediterranean and in Latin America than in, say, England and Germany. A former British official who attended White House meetings with him said, "He's a bit like a spigot that you can turn on and can't turn off." He added, "For all of the genuine charm, it is frustrating that you do feel as if he doesn't leave enough oxygen in the room to get your points across, particularly for those who are polite and don't interrupt." He learned to leave extra room on the schedule to account for what colleagues called "the Biden hour." In Israel, Biden's approach went down better. On a visit in 2011, Biden quoted his father saying, "There's no sense dying on a small cross"—to urge Benjamin Netanyahu to take a larger step toward peace in the Middle East. Ron Dermer, the Israeli ambassador to the U.S. at the time, said, "We're in Jerusalem, we've got a Catholic vice president, we've got a Jewish prime minister, and he's telling him, 'There's no sense dying on a small cross.' The prime minister starting laughing, and, I have to tell you, it is the single most succinct understanding of Israeli political reality of any other statement that I've heard."

Since entering the administration, Biden had been a strident voice of skepticism about the use of American force. At times, that put him on the opposite side of debates from others in the administration, including Hillary Clinton and Panetta, Obama's first CIA director. Biden had opposed intervention in Libya, arguing that the fall of Muammar Qaddafi would result in chaos; Biden had warned the president against the raid that killed Osama bin Laden. If it failed, Biden said later, Obama "would've been a one-term president." Though Obama heeded Biden's advice only sometimes, the two men adhered to a restrained foreign policy that "avoids errors," as Obama put it. Asked to articulate an "Obama doctrine," the president said, "You hit singles, you hit doubles; every once in a while we may be able to hit a home run."

Biden, in contrast to his predecessor, Dick Cheney, made his mark on foreign affairs by reinforcing the president's instincts for restraint, rather than maneuvering around them. In the summer of 2014, I spoke with Obama about Biden's role in the administration. I asked if Biden had influenced his thinking. "On the foreign policy front, I think Joe's biggest influence was in the Afghanistan debate," he said. In 2009, Obama had launched a strategic review of America's policy, and his war cabinet met repeatedly to discuss the best way forward. Military leaders, including the top commander in Afghanistan, General Stanley McChrystal, favored a major counterinsurgency strategy involving forty thousand additional troops and a large civilian force. Obama believed that some of those at the table were predisposed to a specific outcome. He told me, "You had Bob Gates, who proved to be an outstanding secretary of defense, but obviously was somewhat invested in continuity from the previous administration, when it came to Afghanistan policy."

Obama went on, "In the midst of that debate, Joe and I would have lengthy one-on-one conversations, trying to tease out what, precisely, are our interests in Afghanistan, what exactly can we achieve there. I think, in some of the public narratives, it's ended up being framed as Joe being the dove and others being more hawkish. And that, I think, is too simplistic. Really, what Joe helped me to do was to consistently ask the question why, exactly, are we there? And what resources, exactly, can we bring to bear to achieve specific goals?—rather than get caught up in broader ideological debates that all too often end up leading to overreach or a lack of precision in our mission." Obama said that he and Biden discussed questions to pose to the military and intelligence communities. "There were times where Joe would ask questions, essentially on my behalf, to give me decision-making space, to help stir up a vigorous debate. And that was invaluable both in shaping our strategy of an initial surge, to blunt

Taliban momentum, but also to lay out a time frame for how long we would be there. And, you know, to this day there may be, I think, controversy about us imposing a timetable for winding down our combat participation in Afghanistan. I believe it was the absolutely right thing to do." (Obama eventually ordered a civil-military strategy involving thirty thousand additional troops, and America's involvement in Afghanistan continued.)

Some senior leaders at the Pentagon blamed Biden for stoking distrust between the White House and the military. In Gates's memoir, *Duty*, he directed his harshest criticism at Biden. He called him "impossible not to like" but "wrong on nearly every major foreign policy and national security issue over the past four decades." In an interview with National Public Radio about the book, Gates said that Biden had voted against aid to South Vietnam and cheered the fall of the Shah in Iran. "He opposed virtually every element of President Reagan's defense buildup. He voted against the B-1, the B-2, the MX, and so on. He voted against the first Gulf War. So, on a number of these major issues, I just frankly, over a long period of time, felt that he had been wrong."

The conflict between Gates and Biden had a long history. In 1991, when Gates was nominated to be the director of the CIA, Biden voted against him, on the ground that Gates had been a top Kremlinologist at the CIA and failed to anticipate the fall of the Soviet Union. Decades later, when Gates was confirmed as secretary of defense, Biden did not cast a vote. In referring to Biden's errors over "four decades," Gates echoed a conservative talking point produced for the 2008 presidential campaign, when Republicans sought to counter criticism of Sarah Palin's inexperience in foreign affairs. (There is no evidence that Biden spoke approvingly of the fall of the Shah.)

In one of our interviews, Biden brought up the Gates book. "Gates gets upset because I questioned the military. Well, I believe now, believed then, that Washington and Jefferson were all right: war is too important to be left to generals. It is not their judgment to make! Theirs is to execute. So I think you've seen a president who is loyal and supportive of the military but realizes he's the commander in chief." At one point, I started to speak, but Biden interrupted. "I can hardly wait—either in a presidential campaign or when I'm out of here—to debate Bob Gates. Oh, Jesus."

I asked what he made of Gates's specific criticisms. He called Gates "a really decent guy" and then unloaded on him: "Bob Gates is a Republican, with a view of foreign policy that is, in many fundamental ways, different from mine. Bob Gates has been wrong about everything! Bob Gates is wrong about the advice he gave President Reagan about how to deal with [Soviet leader Mikhail]

Gorbachev! That he wasn't real. Thank God the president didn't listen to him. Bob Gates was wrong about the Balkans. Bob Gates was wrong about the [NATO] bombing [there]. Bob Gates was wrong about the Vietnam War, for Christ's sake. You go back, and everything in the last forty years, there's nothing that I can think of, major fundamental decisions relative to foreign policy, that I can think he's been right about!"

The tenor of the dispute between Biden and Gates surprised some who know them. When I asked Richard Haass, the president of the Council on Foreign Relations, about Gates's assessment of Biden, Haass said, "Bob Gates is a close friend. We worked together in government several times, but it's one of the areas where I disagree with him. Nobody bats a thousand, but I don't know anyone who bats zero, either. Joe's had his hits and he's had his misses, just like the rest of us." Panetta, who served alongside Gates and Biden, said the two frequently clashed during the debates that Obama had engineered to draw out disagreement. Over time, Panetta said, Gates was alienated by Biden's questioning of his assumptions. "It just kind of ate away at him," Panetta said.

Back on Air Force Two for the trip home, Biden loosened his tie and asked for a cup of coffee. Before departing Kiev, he had ad-libbed a poke at Russia's pledge to reduce tensions: "Stop talking and start acting." In New

York, Senator John McCain heard that and said, "Or else what?"—a criticism of the Obama administration for not moving more forcefully against Russia.

Ukrainian officials had appealed to the United States for military support, but Biden had advised them that it would be minimal, if at all. He told me, "We no longer think in Cold War terms, for several reasons. One, no one is our equal. No one is close. Other than being crazy enough to press a button, there is nothing that Putin can do militarily to fundamentally alter American interests." The Ukrainians were not pleased. A senior administration official said, "My read of the looks on their faces was 'Holy God.'"

Biden was determined not to get the United States drawn into a regional conflict; he had no illusions about Putin's intentions. He was still alarmed, more than a decade later, by George W. Bush's misreading in 2001, that Putin was "very straightforward and trustworthy." Bush said he "was able to get a sense of his soul; a man deeply committed to his country and the best interests of his country." Biden recalled visiting Putin at the Kremlin in 2011: "I had an interpreter, and when he was showing me his office I said, 'It's amazing what capitalism will do, won't it? A magnificent office!' And he laughed. As I turned, I was this close to him." Biden held his hand a few inches from his nose. "I said, 'Mr. Prime Minister,

I'm looking into your eyes, and I don't think you *have* a soul.'"

"You said that?" I asked. It sounded like a movie line.

"Absolutely, positively," Biden said, and continued, "And he looked back at me, and he smiled, and he said, 'We understand one another.'" Biden sat back, and exclaimed, "This is who this guy is!"

That summer, I arranged to tail Biden to some meetings. One afternoon, he crossed the strip of asphalt between the West Wing and the Eisenhower Executive Office Building, home to what's known as his Ceremonial Office, used for groups too large for his space in the White House. Climbing the steps, we talked about Richard Ben Cramer's profile of Biden in *What It Takes*. Biden had been vaguely unsettled by a fond but unsparing portrait of his rise and fall in the 1988 campaign. (Cramer emphasized Biden's "breathtaking element of balls . . . more balls than sense.") "It's embarrassing when someone shows you something about yourself that you didn't already know," Biden said. But, when Cramer died, in 2013, Biden delivered a eulogy. We reached the top of the steps, and Biden, a bit winded, stopped to think about why Cramer's portrait affected him. "He used this word—he said, 'Biden never does something unless he can "see" it.' And he was absolutely right. I never do anything I can't 'see.' "

The crisis in Ukraine had hardened into a bitter stalemate. Members of the Obama administration turned gingerly back to the many other foreign policy problems that confronted them. In Biden's Ceremonial Office, two dozen visitors were seated around a long table, ready to discuss Cyprus, which has been divided since 1974, when Turkey invaded it to prevent the island from unifying with Greece. Cyprus wanted U.S. help in resolving the standoff and in tapping oil and gas deposits. In late May, Biden had made the most senior visit by a U.S. official since Vice President Lyndon Johnson, in 1962, and his guests that afternoon were Greek American leaders he had known for years. One of them told Biden he looked skinny. "I'm working at it! I'm down to one-seventy-nine and I'm ready to fight!" he said, the latest in a growing patter about a potential campaign in 2016.

During the meeting, Biden was at full sail; he gave a high-energy review of his trip, reenacted his meetings, whispered in confidence, threw his hands skyward, vowed to find a resolution for a conflict that had dragged on, as he said, for "forty goddamn years, man!" He worked up a sweat and peeled off his suit jacket. After half an hour, Biden was supposed to leave, and a staffer who guarded his schedule passed him a folded note. Biden looked at it and kept right on talking. Thirty more minutes went by. The staffer edged around the table to stand in his line of sight. Finally, sixty-four minutes after he arrived, having talked for about fifty-five of them, Biden announced that he had to go back to Ukraine, this time to attend the presidential inauguration. A member of the group, Andy Manatos, a Greek American lobbyist, thanked him for his attention to Cyprus, saying that this was "probably the first time in forty years that we trust where our administration wants to go on this." On the way out, Manatos stopped and said to me, "You've heard of the Lyndon Johnson treatment? That was the Biden treatment."

When Biden placed phone calls from the White House to people he knew, he occasionally skipped the White House operator, dialed direct, and caught them unprepared. On formal calls with foreign leaders, he stuck to the protocol, but tried to work in some friendly chitchat—grandkids, food, weather. That summer, White House phone records showed that Biden had placed more calls to Iraq—sixty-four of them, to be exact—than to any other country. Throughout the Obama administration, Iraq had been one of Biden's most consuming preoccupations.

In his Senate years, Biden had never maintained a uniform view of the use of force. In 1991, he had voted against the Gulf War, but, in 1993, he advocated the NATO air strikes in the Balkans to stop the Serbian slaughter of Bosnians, which he viewed as one of his proudest moments. In 2002, during the run-up to the war in Iraq, he pushed a resolution that would have allowed Bush to remove weapons of mass destruction in Iraq but not to remove Saddam Hussein. The resolution failed, and Biden voted for the war, a decision he came to regret.

Biden never had much confidence in Iraq's political coherence. In the spring of 2006, he happened to sit next to Leslic Gelb, the former head of the Council on Foreign Relations, on a flight from New York to Washington. The flight was delayed, Gelb said, and "for three hours we talked and talked, only about Iraq." They hatched an idea for a federal system incorporating three semiautonomous regions, for Shiites, Sunnis, and Kurds, based partly on Biden's experience with the division of Bosnia. They published the idea in an op-ed in *The New York Times* in May 2006. "It got a lot of attention—almost all negative," Gelb recalled. Foreign policy commentators said that it would lead Iraq to disintegration, or, worse, ethnic cleansing. "I watched this with great interest to see how Joe would react," Gelb said. "Because, under that kind of pressure, with everybody telling you, 'You're wrong,' politicians just run for the hills. He never did at all. Not one iota." (I later asked Michael O'Hanlon, a foreign policy expert at the Brookings Institution, his view of the proposed federal system. He said, "It's not a crazy idea, it never was crazy, and it may still be a necessary fallback.")

Not long after the 2008 election, Rahm Emanuel, then the incoming chief of staff, met with Obama to parcel out assignments—especially on the delicate matter of the faltering war in Iraq. "You needed somebody who was loyal to the marrow with their vote," Emanuel told me, "wasn't looking for glory, and knew all the different factions—not just in our government but also in the Iraq government, and who had no filter to the Oval Office." Biden fit the bill. At a national security meeting in June 2009, Obama turned to Biden and said, unceremoniously, "Joe, you do Iraq." To the administration's critics, that handoff was a sign of Obama's disregard for what he considered the "dumb war" (as compared to the "good war," in Afghanistan).

Three years after he had proposed a plan that would give Iraq greater regional autonomy, Biden was now tasked with keeping the country together. To that end, he supported the government led by Prime Minister Nuri al-Maliki; he asked a rival, Ayad Allawi, to drop his bid for prime minister and accept a lower position. Despite growing concern among American diplomats and allies in the region that the Iraqi prime minister was an increasingly sectarian and despotic figure, Biden considered Maliki the only viable option. He invoked his belief in the power of rational interests, as an ingredient in politics. Panetta said, "I remember Joe basically saying to al-Maliki, 'This is in your political interest. You want to run that country? You want to be able to go down in history as somebody who was able to save that country? It's going to be critical to your legacy.'"

Biden was optimistic; he predicted that a stable, representative government in Baghdad was "going to be one of the great achievements of this administration," as he said in 2010. He predicted that Maliki would sign on to a Status of Forces Agreement, which would allow a contingent of U.S. troops to stay in Iraq. "I'll bet you my vice presidency Maliki will extend the SOFA," he reportedly told other administration officials, during a video conference. But that confidence had proved misplaced. In 2011, Maliki refused to heed American requests, and the U.S. ended the effort to leave forces in Iraq. In December, Biden visited Baghdad to mark the American withdrawal. He called Obama and thanked him "for giving me the chance to end this goddamn war." The bluster was premature.

In June 2014, I paid a call on Biden in his West Wing office. Less than three years after he'd hailed the end of that goddamn war, Sunni militants calling themselves ISIS—for the Islamic State in Iraq and al-Sham—took control of Mosul, the country's second-largest city, and Obama prepared to send the first of thousands of troops back to Iraq. The border between Iraq and Syria was collapsing, and two wars, once distinct, were merging.

In shirtsleeves, Biden slumped onto a blue couch in front of his desk, and gave a theatrical sigh of weariness. For years, a mix of critics on both the left and the right had pressed the administration to take greater steps in Syria, to save human life or to blunt the strategic chaos now rippling across the region. I asked him if the U.S. could have done anything differently in Syria. For fifteen seconds, Biden said nothing. Finally, he said, "Yeah, maybe." In 2012, the White House rejected a CIA-backed plan to arm moderate rebels, for fear that it would draw the United States into the conflict and put weapons into the wrong hands. After Syria's president, Bashar al-Assad, was found to have used chemical weapons in June 2013, Obama authorized the effort. America's goal, Biden said, was to remove Assad without unleashing a sectarian civil war. But, he said, "I did not think and did not believe our allies were on the same page." Leaders of Qatar, Saudi Arabia, and other regional powers were arming Sunni jihadists whom the United States was unwilling to support. "I believed it was critically important that the Qataris, the Emiratis, the Saudis, the Turks all decide on who were the little guys," he said. "Who were we going to support? Were we committed to leaving in place a government intact you could rebuild, and not end up with a divided country?"

Biden recalled telling the Emir of Qatar, over breakfast in April 2013, "You guys can't continue to just fund the most radical Islamists there." The vice president believed that foreign powers were turning the conflict into "more of a proxy war for Sunni and Shia." Biden said, "You can't be sending in tens of millions of dollars to al-Nusra"—an Islamist terrorist group—"and say that 'we're on the same page.' Because it's not gonna end well." He sat back. "To the extent that there was the possibility of having this end well, sooner, it was the failure of the ability to generate a unanimity of consensus."

Before I could ask Biden about what had led to this moment, he offered a defense of his record of arguing against the use of force. "Look, one thing I feel certain about is that this has nothing to do with if we had thirty thousand troops there, or if we had sixty or ten." He drew a comparison to Afghanistan. "Both of these countries, coming out of really difficult circumstances, we gave them an opportunity. A chance. Offered them space and time." He was pessimistic about the spiraling chaos in Syria and Iraq, but he maintained the belief that the

U.S. would be wrong to try to wrestle the parties into submission or agreement. "Notwithstanding all of the hundreds of hours I and others spent with each of their leaders, they didn't resolve a core problem of how the hell they're gonna live together. And it wouldn't have mattered if we stayed there."

Few American commanders or diplomats lamented the end of a grueling U.S. occupation, but some criticized Biden for investing so much in Maliki, or for not pushing harder to leave a force that might have preserved American influence and checked Maliki's sectarian project. When Biden and I talked about Iraq, he had spoken to Maliki a day earlier, and he no longer bothered to voice confidence in him: "The good and bad news is this has happened at a propitious time, because they're in the government-formation phase now, and what you may very well see is, among the Shia, a decision that, maybe, Maliki is not the guy to carry the mail." Biden expressed only a limited ambition to bring a resolution to Iraq. He said, "We can't want unity and coherence, even though it's overwhelmingly in our interest, more than they want it."

That summer, as the government in Baghdad drifted deeper into dysfunction, Biden's old notion of a federal decentralized Iraq went from a radical proposal to a blunt acknowledgment of reality. Stratfor, the intelligence-analysis firm, predicted that Iraq "will largely behave as a confederation over time." Almost nobody was pretending that this was a desirable outcome. Zalmay Khalilzad and Kenneth Pollack, Iraq experts at the Center for Strategic & International Studies and the Brookings Institution, called it the "best—or perhaps just the least bad" option at the moment.

As Biden entered the final quarter of the Obama presidency, the chemistry of the White House was changing. After nearly four years as secretary of state, Hillary Clinton had stepped down in 2013; she had maintained a grueling travel schedule, visiting more countries than anyone else who had served in the post, and had suffered a concussion and blood clot that sidelined her for a month. She was succeeded by John Kerry. He had a good relationship with Biden, though their skills and experience overlapped, leaving Biden less in demand on foreign affairs. Unlike Clinton, Kerry had arrived in the job after decades of foreign policy experience in the Senate, and, like Biden, he maintained long-standing relationships with foreign leaders. Moreover, the talk of the 2016 election was building. Biden took pride in his contributions to the administration: a voice in favor of ending two wars, no matter how unresolved; attempts to reckon with a nonfunctioning Congress; a show of support for the rights of gays and lesbians, even at the cost of his relations with Obama's political advisers. He knew that his take on his legacy would be contested; Bob Gates was only the first to put down his marker.

As we wound down one of our interviews, Biden said of the vice presidency, "For all my skepticism about taking the job, it's been the most worthwhile thing I've ever done in my life." He rose and put on a navy blue suit jacket, and gave a slight shot of his cuffs. He was due at a national security meeting. Biden knew that others—especially Hillary Clinton—wondered about his intentions in the presidential race, but he was no in rush to share them. When I asked about it, he gave the ritual denials, and said, "I can die a happy man not being president."

I called one of Biden's friends to run it by him. He laughed: "For six years, I've been saying, if you don't believe that Joe Biden intends to run in 2016, you don't know Joe Biden."

CHAPTER 6

The Lucky
and the Unlucky

When Biden signed on as a running mate in 2008, he told Obama, "I'm sixty-five and you're not going to have to worry about my positioning myself to be President." If Obama served two terms, and Biden managed to succeed him, he would have been the oldest new president in history.

But by 2011, he was reconsidering the idea; he started convening strategy sessions at the Naval Observatory, the vice president's official residence, with family and long-time political aides: Ted Kaufman, Ron Klain, and others. The first time I asked Biden about it, in early 2014, he offered the ritual denials: "My job's about the president. I know this sounds silly, but I really mean it. I have one job. One job: help this man, whom I admire greatly, finish his term by getting as much done on an agenda that I share, and I believe in." When I pressed, he said, "Somewhere between a day and six or eight months after the congressional elections"—in the fall of 2014—"it will be the issue, whether I'm in it or not."

The truth was that Biden already faced a predicament that was all but unprecedented in modern American politics; in the past half century, every sitting vice president who sought the presidency had won his party's nomination. But, even a year before Hillary Clinton formally announced her candidacy, Biden was trailing her in polls by margins of 50 points or more. If she did not run, or if she stumbled, Biden could step in. For the moment, though, he was in limbo—finding ways to stay in the picture, help his president, and burnish his legacy.

When I talked to him about the decision to retire or run again, he brought up his father. "I made a mistake in encouraging him to retire. I just think as long as you think you can do it and you're physically healthy—" He changed tack. "I actually had the discussion with Barack. I said, 'Look, I'm not going to be out there like Al [Gore], going to everybody's birthday in Iowa.' I'm not going to do that. But, you know, I've not made a decision I'm *not* going to do this."

More than a year before the Iowa caucuses of 2016, Biden's prospects were not good. Even though he was a frequent visitor to South Carolina (home of the third primary), a 2012 poll had found that nearly a third of those surveyed there couldn't name the sitting vice president. And, yet, as a short-term strategy, Biden's stage whispers about the presidency were serving him well. A vice president who avidly pursued the top job was a distraction. But Biden was staving off lame-duck status by stoking speculation about his willingness to complicate a Clinton candidacy. Even if Biden could not yet see a viable route to the nomination, leaving that prospect on the table kept him in the deal. One of his aides told me that Biden saw himself as "the shark that has to keep swimming to stay alive." In less dire terms, Dennis Toner, who worked on Biden's staff for more than thirty years, said, "This is what your whole life's been about. Then how, at this point, do you walk away?"

The longer I spent with Biden, the more I noticed how often he returned to questions of respect—in his childhood, in his father's struggles, in the ancient slights and courtesies that he had suffered on his way up. Respect is a permanent feature in political psychology (in an episode of *Veep*, Julia Louis-Dreyfus was expounding on its importance—"You know the Aretha Franklin song"—when she walked into a plate glass door), but Biden's old-neighborhood sensibilities elevated it to a sacred position. I concluded that, for Biden, running for president was less important than confirming that people afforded him the respect of taking it seriously.

Biden and Hillary Clinton had a friendship that dated to the 1992 Clinton campaign. She liked to say that he reminded her of her husband—two folksy bootstrappers with politics in their bone marrow—and, when she reached the Senate, Biden and Clinton shared rides on Amtrak. After she delivered an impassioned endorsement for Obama and Biden at the Democratic National Convention, in 2008, Biden found her backstage, dropped to his knees in gratitude, and kissed her hand. He enthusiastically backed her selection as secretary of state. In the administration, they differed sharply on the use of American force; she favored a surge in Afghanistan, a mission to depose Qaddafi, and the bin Laden raid, and he opposed all three. Nevertheless, they kept a standing Tuesday breakfast at his residence, with no staff. He made a point to meet her at her car and walk her to a sunny nook off the porch. "Always the gentleman," she wrote in *Hard Choices*, her memoir of her years in the administration. He sometimes signed off his phone calls to her, "I love you, darling."

It was hard to overstate Clinton's advantage. For twelve consecutive years, she had been the most admired woman in America, according to Gallup. (As of 2014, Michelle Obama was No. 3, behind Oprah, and tied with Sarah Palin.) Ready for Hillary, a political action committee, had raised over $8.3 million more than two years before the election. Biden had no fund-raising infrastructure. Writing for *The Atlantic* in 2014, Peter Beinart took stock of Clinton's momentum and concluded, "Joe Biden's prospective Presidential candidacy is in danger of becoming a joke." Beinart mourned that development, arguing that the contrast between Biden and Clinton could spark a productive debate about the Democratic Party's direction on issues including "America's role in the world."

Ed Rendell, the former governor and Democratic Party official, was a Biden friend and a Clinton supporter. That spring, I asked him what kind of challenge Biden could mount against Clinton. "He can't, because his political supporters and his financial supporters are all for Hillary," Rendell said. "The response they would give him is 'Joe, I love you, I think you'd make a fine President, but it's Hillary's time.' Joe happens to be standing in the way of history." But if Clinton did not run, or faltered, Rendell added, Biden could well attract more Democratic support than was immediately apparent: "If Hillary pulled out on Tuesday, I would call Joe on Wednesday and say, 'Whatever you want me to do.'

And I think that 60 to 70 percent of the Hillary people feel the same."

Campaigns move in unpredictable directions, and, that summer, Clinton made a series of clumsy comments about her wealth; she said that her family was "dead broke" when it left the White House, and that she and Bill Clinton were not "truly well off," even as she was touring the country giving paid speeches. Biden, by contrast, had taken to making comments that might position him as a more progressive alternative, à la Senator Elizabeth Warren. "I have a basic disagreement," he told me, "with the underlying rationale that began in the Clinton administration about the concentration of economic wealth to generate economic growth." The middle class, he said, was "getting clobbered." He went on, "I think there has to be a significant change in both, over time, fiscal policy and tax policy." He was trying to get that view "further insinuated into the White House," he said. It seemed like boilerplate, and I didn't write about it at the time. That was a mistake. He was describing an emerging divide in the Democratic Party over the degree to which it needed to address the frustrations of working-class voters, especially whites, some of whom eventually turned to Bernie Sanders—and others to Trump.

Biden continued, "I'll be blunt with you: the only vote I can think of that I've ever cast in my years in the

Senate that I regret—and I did it out of loyalty, and I wasn't aware that it was gonna be as bad as it was—was Glass-Steagall." The 1999 repeal of the Glass-Steagall Act, which once separated commercial and investment banking, partially facilitated the 2008 financial crisis. (Over the years, Biden has expressed regret about other votes, including his support for the invasion of Iraq and for tougher sentencing on the possession of crack cocaine.)

In public, he was staking out a populist economic appeal that put him squarely to Clinton's left. At the time, Sanders was still months away from entering the presidential race, and Biden was developing a pitch that would serve him if he ran. He told a union audience that Ken Langone, the billionaire cofounder of Home Depot, had complained about Pope Francis's critique of income inequity. Biden said of Langone, "As a practicing Catholic, bless me, Father, for he has sinned." He warned members of the United Auto Workers that conservatives had launched "a concerted, full-throated, well-organized, well-financed, well-thought-out effort waging war on labor's house."

As Clinton fended off further questions about her income, Biden told an audience in Washington that he was wearing a "mildly expensive suit," despite not owning "a single stock or bond." (To be precise, his family kept securities in his wife's name.) On Comedy Central, Jon Stewart declared it "a good old-fashioned Poor-Off."

In his office that day, the more Biden talked about a possible campaign, the more animated he got about the prospect of running as an economic populist. He stood up from the couch and rooted around his desk for something. He had recently dug up his 2008 convention speech and was struck by how many issues remain unresolved. He located it in the piles on his desk, and standing in the middle of the office, he leafed through the pages. "There is a line in it that I use, that I say, 'I'm running for cops, firemen, nurses, teachers, and assembly-line workers.'" He said people ask him, "'Biden, why do you keep talking about income inequity and all of that?' I go back and look at my speech: it's why the hell I was running!" He stared at me, smiling broadly, still standing. "We're not talking enough about income inequality," he said. "We're not talking enough about how in God's name could you talk about a $5.7 trillion additional tax cut, for Christ's sake. How can we continue to say a 20 percent tax on carried interest is fair? Why the hell aren't we talking about earned income versus unearned income?"

By Jill Biden's count, she had participated in thirteen political campaigns for her husband and for her stepson

Beau. I had been told by others that members of Biden's family were reluctant to embark on another campaign. When I asked her if she thought her husband would run again, she offered no hint of hesitation, saying that they would see "how things evolve," but added that life in office leaves little time to discuss the future. After a series of events the previous night, she said, "We went upstairs, we got out our briefing books. You have to brief for the next day. It's a lifestyle. It's something you never leave. It's not just a job; it's not a job you go to and come home from. You live it; you breathe it."

When I interviewed Obama that summer, I mentioned that he had praised Clinton's attributes as a potential president and asked what he thought of Biden's prospects. "I think Joe would be a superb president," Obama said. "He has seen the job up close, he knows what the job entails. He understands how to separate what's really important from what's less important. I think he's got great people skills. He enjoys politics, and he's got important relationships up on the Hill that would serve him well." I happened to catch Obama at a moment of restlessness. After six years cloistered in the White House, he had taken to comparing himself to a caged animal. A few hours after we spoke, he took an unexpected walk to Starbucks, telling reporters, "The bear is loose." In that vein, Obama couldn't hide his bewilderment that two of his friends would want to subject themselves to another presidential campaign. "I think that, for both Joe and for Hillary, they've already accomplished an awful lot in their lives. The question is, do they, at this phase in their lives, want to go through the pretty undignifying process of running all over again."

Obama returned to the subject of Biden. "You have to have that fire in the belly, which is a question that only Joe can answer himself." He added, "In the meantime, what I'm very grateful for is that he has not let that question infect our relationship or how he has operated as vice president. He continues to be extraordinarily loyal. He continues to take on big assignments that may not have a huge political upside.

"You know, when I sent him to Ukraine for the recent inauguration of Poroshenko, and he's there, a world figure that people know, and he's signifying the importance that we place on the Ukrainian election," Obama went on. "And then world leaders can transmit directly to him their thoughts about how we proceed. That's not necessarily helping him in Iowa."

When I asked Biden how he would decide to run for president, he ticked off the factors: the motivation ("Do you really believe you have the capacity to change things that you're passionate about?"), the chances ("Can you win this thing?"), the organization ("Can I raise a billion dollars?"), the family ("If Jill were not happy—it sounds like a stupid thing—but I'm not happy.").

I asked Biden how he would respond if opponents say he was too old to be president. "I think it's totally legitimate for people to raise it," he said. "And I'll just say, 'Look at me. Decide.'" He went on, "How I measure somebody, whether it's playing sports, running a company, or in public life, is how much passion they still have. How much they tackle the job. I mean, *tackle* it." He knocked on a wooden side table beside the sofa and said, "I know from experience I could be ill. I could be a cancer victim or have a heart attack. That's another reason why my dad used to say, 'Never argue with your wife about something that's going to happen more than a year from now.'"

To a degree unknown to the public at the time, Biden's personal life was changing in a way that would shadow his remaining years in the White House. In the summer of 2013, his son Beau (Joseph Robinette Biden III), who was the attorney general of Delaware and a father of two, had been diagnosed as having glioblastoma, an aggressive form of brain cancer. Father and son were unusually close; he was a confidant and protégé, and even as a teenager, Beau had played an influential role in his father's political life, standing close enough during speeches to offer whispered advice. Richard Ben Cramer, in *What It Takes*, recalled an event during Biden's failing 1987 campaign. The crowd was so quiet that you "could hear wool pants rustling on Naugahyde banquet chairs," Cramer wrote. As the listeners peeled away, Biden was still talking at full tilt, "till Beau, toward the end, was staring at his shoes, murmuring, 'Dad . . . finish.'" For years, the father told friends that Beau had "all of my best qualities and none of my worst."

After the diagnosis, Beau entered a grueling regimen of surgery and experimental treatments. In a highly personal book about those years, *Promise Me, Dad*, Biden recalled telling Obama that he planned to take out a second mortgage, to cover the mounting bills. "Don't do that," Obama said. "I'll give you the money. I have it. You can pay me back whenever." (Biden never took him up on it.)

Along the way, there were moments of false hope. In one of our interviews, he stepped away to take a phone call and returned, smiling, his eyes glistening. "Just got really good family news," he said. I asked if he wanted to take a break.

"Ah, no, I just—I just can't tell you how good I feel," he said.

Afterward, an aide explained that the good news was

about the progress of Beau's treatment. But the optimism was short-lived. On May 30, 2015, Beau died, at the age of forty-six. In his diary that night, Biden wrote, "It happened. My God, my boy. My beautiful boy."

The anguish cut especially deep in the culture of the Biden family, a clan that prided itself on a fierce solidarity. Biden sometimes talked of his people in anthropological terms—"We Bidens," he'd say. ("We Bidens have strong personalities, and we live close," he wrote.) When I once showed up for an interview at his office, he appeared to be in mid-thought. It was a busy week—I was there to talk to him about Iraq, Ukraine, and other dramas—but when I asked what he'd been thinking about at his desk, he beamed. "A First Communion, man!" It was coming up that weekend, in Delaware, and Biden was heading home. "I look around at my sister, and a lot of my peers, and younger peers with children who are getting out of college, and they're scattered all over the universe. I've really been lucky." He said, "Every Sunday, when we're home, we have dinner, you know. It's been that way for twenty-five years."

After the news broke of Beau's death, Obama praised Beau for "a life that was full; a life that mattered." In a comment directed to Joe and Jill, he added, "The Bidens have more family than they know." There was something to that. Even as the Biden family edged into privilege, its tragedy, its striving, and its improbable optimism had made it stick out as a more approachable American clan than the Kennedys or the Clintons or the Obamas.

Among the tributes to the Bidens, Senator Harry Reid said, "There's a song, 'A Man of Constant Sorrow,' that, certainly, if that ever applied to someone, it would be our friend Joe Biden." The sentiment was kind, but, to people close to Biden, the analogy sounds just a few degrees off of true. The Bidens' sorrow, after all, was exceptional, but never constant. Biden's friend Ted Kaufman told me, "If you ask me who's the unluckiest person I know personally, who's had just terrible things happen to him, I'd say Joe Biden. If you asked me who is the luckiest person I know personally, who's had things happen to him that are just absolutely incredible, I'd say Joe Biden."

For decades, Biden had a fitful relationship with his public connection to suffering. Long after the car crash, he talked about it only occasionally; he worried how people would respond; and vulnerability clashed with the bluff style of his generation. But after his son's death, aides saw a change. "The whole Beau experience just killed off the arrogant stuff," a former colleague told me. "It was almost physical. You could see it in how he stood.

He wasn't the old college football player anymore. He emerged as this sort of humbled, purposeful man."

In the fall of 2015, Biden went on *The Late Show*, hosted by Stephen Colbert. They had some shared experience: when Colbert was a child, his father and two brothers died in a plane crash. Before the taping, they met alone backstage. "It was one of the most compact and affecting conversations I think I've ever had," Colbert told me. During the interview, Biden talked about mourning his son, struggling to retain his composure. Colbert, informed by his own experience, saw a purpose in putting that anguish in public view. "Very few people want to approach grief, and not only their own grief, but anyone else's grief," he told me. "I think there is some sense that grief is contagious. Joe Biden does not have that. He expresses the loneliness of grief and makes you feel less alone," he told me. "For all of his mid-century American male qualities, he is not burdened with a particular curse of not being able to share any sense of weakness or injury."

Biden's association with pain and resilience at times puts him outside the usual bounds of retail politics. "People come up to him, and this is all they want to talk about: 'How do I get through it?'" Mike Donilon, his chief strategist, said. When Biden and Obama worked a rope line, Biden sometimes took so long that aides had to restart the soundtrack. Reporters and operatives joked that this was Biden's timeworn shtick, lingering too long for pictures and gabbing about his team, the Phillies. People who have worked with him describe it differently. "The music will be blaring, and people will be screaming for a selfie, and some staff person will be pushing him on, and he will just stop," Donilon said. "He will sit there, and he will talk to this person."

In the years that Biden was managing Beau's decline, his other son, Hunter, was in crisis of a different kind. For decades, Hunter had struggled with addiction to drugs and alcohol, which he once described as "a never-ending tunnel." In February 2014, he was discharged from the Navy Reserve after testing positive for cocaine. His marriage was failing, and he later had a brief relationship with Beau's widow. Along the way, Republicans who were eager to undermine Biden's candidacy promoted the notion, without evidence, that Biden had used his power to help Hunter's businesses in China and Ukraine. Over the years, Hunter had worked at a bank, a lobbying firm, and a hedge fund, but his father kept his distance, to avoid accusations of a conflict of interest.

That distance was becoming harder to maintain. In the spring of 2014, at the same time that Biden was playing a central role in overseeing U.S. policy in Ukraine, Hunter joined the board of Burisma, one of Ukraine's largest natural gas producers. His decision to take the board position bothered members of the Obama administration; Hunter's position had no effect on policy, they insisted, but it looked unseemly. For several years, Hunter was in and out of substance abuse treatment, while mourning his brother and pursuing business deals. After he crashed a rental car in Arizona, a worker recovered a crack pipe and found Beau Biden's attorney general badge on the dashboard. Hunter later told Adam Entous, of *The New Yorker*, that his father discussed Burisma with him only once: "Dad said, 'I hope you know what you are doing,' and I said, 'I do.'" (Hunter later apologized to him, and said publicly it was "poor judgment" to have joined the board. He vowed not to work for any foreign companies if his father became president.)

Even as Biden contended with Beau's death, and Hunter's struggles, Washington speculation was building around Biden's potential run for the presidency. In Washington, people debated how he would fare against Hillary Clinton, in a race for the Democratic nomination. In the typical analysis, she had various advantages: she was five years younger, broadly popular within her party, with a growing mountain of campaign funds—not to mention, the prospect that she would make history, as the first woman president.

There was another important factor: it was increasingly apparent to Biden that Obama saw Clinton as his natural successor. Previously, the signs had been subtle. In 2014, during a routine interview with *CBS This Morning*, Biden and Obama were side by side when the reporter, Major Garrett, asked about the 2016 race. Obama lavished praise upon Biden as "a great partner in everything I do." Then Obama began to talk about someone else: "I suspect that there may be other potential candidates for 2016 who have been great friends and allies. We've got an extraordinary secretary of state who did great service for us, for me and Joe." Biden looked away for an instant, and then back toward the president, with a strained smile. It was no endorsement of Hillary Clinton. It was nothing—unless you saw it.

In their private dealings, Obama was "subtly weighing in against—for a variety of reasons," Biden wrote later. A tough internal contest would detract public focus from the administration's final year of work, and it risked splitting the party into factions that would be weaker against a Republican opponent. Besides, he wrote, with a trace of irritation, Obama was "convinced I could not beat Hillary." Biden wondered if Obama had already promised Clinton he would support her, but he did not want it to come between the two men. "I got it, and never took issue with him," Biden wrote. "This was about Barack's legacy, and a significant portion of that legacy had not yet been cast in stone."

Biden's advisers saw it very differently. They cited polls that showed Biden with higher levels of favorability than many candidates of either party, including potential Republican frontrunners at the time, Jeb Bush and Marco Rubio. Though Biden was polling far behind Clinton in New Hampshire, he led her in key states, such as Florida, Ohio, and Pennsylvania. And, he registered high scores on character qualities such as honesty and empathy. The surprise early success of Bernie Sanders suggested that Biden's talk of income inequality, and reviving labor unions, might find support, though Biden would need to move fast to claim that territory.

By the fall of 2016, Biden was still mourning his son, and struggling over the decision to run or not. He had raised no money, hired no staff, and created no organization in the states. At a meeting with advisers and family, Donilon saw the pain etched on his face and said, finally, "I don't think you should do this." Donilon had been among the most fervent advocates for entering the race. "I believe he could've won," he told me later. "I looked at him that night at the vice president's house, and he just looked to be in too much pain. He couldn't go."

In the Rose Garden the next day, October 21, with Jill and Obama at his side, Biden announced that he would not run for president. He tried to present a sense of certainty, but his ambivalence was unmistakable. "While I will not be a candidate, I will not be silent," he said. "I intend to speak out clearly and forcefully to influence as much as I can where we stand as a party and where we need to go as a nation." He spoke from just a few notes. It was slow and patient, by his standards. He directed his comments not only to the public, but also to his colleagues in Washington. He beseeched them to "end the divisive partisan politics that is ripping this country apart." He said, "Four more years of this kind of pitched battle may be more than this country can take."

It was, it seemed, the end of a five-decade dream, reaching back to his boyhood boast to Neilia's mother that he would be president someday. He had run his last race, or so it appeared. But Biden's life had often turned in directions that were difficult to predict, and it was about to turn once more.

CHAPTER 7

Battle for the Soul

In the summer of 2017, Biden was in semiretirement, working to support cancer research and telling anyone in earshot that he could have beaten Trump.

That August, after white supremacists carried torches through Charlottesville, Virginia, Biden watched as Trump spoke approvingly of the "very fine people" on both sides. "I thought, Holy God, this guy is going to be so much worse than I thought he was," Biden told me. He read *How Democracies Die*, by the Harvard political scientists Steven Levitsky and Daniel Ziblatt, and heard echoes of it in the headlines. "Look what's being done. Look what's being said. Not just by him but by his followers and some of his elected colleagues," Biden said. Trump's actions played on a reservoir of existing anger, he thought: "It didn't just happen with Trump. I'm not even sure Trump understands it."

Many of Biden's primary opponents—notably Sanders and Warren—were running forthrightly progressive campaigns: a Green New Deal, Medicare for All, free public college, decriminalized borders. They were winning widespread support, especially among young people. By the end of this decade, millennials and Generation Z are on pace to constitute a majority of America's eligible voters. In 2018, twenty millennials were elected to Congress, including Alexandria Ocasio-Cortez, a Sanders supporter and a democratic socialist who upset a powerful moderate Democrat in the Bronx.

But Biden believed that his peers had missed a crucial lesson of the midterm elections: forty-three House districts had moved from Republicans to Democrats, as some older, moderate voters recoiled from Trump's party. "We won by not going after the opponent but after the issues underlying what the opponent supported," he told me. "They were running against Obamacare, and all of a sudden you heard them say, 'I didn't say I was for doing away with *that*.'" Biden had a chance with some fed-up Trump voters, according to Samuel Popkin, a veteran pollster and the author of *Crackup*, about the divisions within the Republican Party. "Farm bankruptcy is near the highest it's been in thirty years," Popkin said. In 2018, Trump flew to Wisconsin, promising what he called the "eighth wonder of the world"—a factory to be built for

Foxconn, the Taiwanese electronics company. "Foxconn barely built anything in Wisconsin," Popkin said.

In planning his campaign, Biden focused on reforms that stopped well short of revolution. Instead of Medicare for All, he wanted to augment Obamacare, by lowering the Medicare eligibility age from sixty-five to sixty, and adding a "public option"—an idea that was considered radical a decade ago but is now conservative by the new standards. His campaign cited polls showing that a majority of potential Democratic primary voters identified as moderate or conservative, and more than half were over the age of fifty. "The young left is important," Anita Dunn, a top Biden adviser, told me. "But so are older white people above the age of sixty-five, because they actually gave the election to Donald Trump last time."

Biden's candidacy rested on a bet that, when the pendulum of history swung away from Trump, it might swing toward experience and incrementalism, rather than toward youth and progressive zeal. Biden was seeking to persuade Americans that his experience of working-class life and of personal loss and suffering outweighed the liabilities. In a supremely odd way, Trump had already testified to Biden's potential strength as a candidate. Since 2018, conservatives such as Rudolph Giuliani, Trump's personal lawyer, had been seeking media attention for what Giuliani called an "alleged Ukraine conspiracy," accusing Biden, without evidence, of firing Ukraine's prosecutor general to thwart investigations into Hunter and the gas company Burisma. In July 2019, in a now famous phone call with Ukraine's leader Volodymyr Zelensky, Trump asked Zelensky to "do us a favor" and investigate the Bidens. Once the contents of that call were revealed by a whistleblower, Trump, in December, became the third president in American history to be impeached by the House of Representatives. Trump, who maintained that his behavior was "perfect," was acquitted by the Republican majority in the Senate. Biden, for his part, was bewildered by an episode that, he hoped, bespoke both Trump's frailty and his own prospects. "He decided he didn't want me as a nominee," he told me.

In the spring of 2019, just before Biden announced his candidacy, he ran headlong into his past—and the widening gap in sensibilities between generations. Lucy Flores, a former Nevada state legislator, published an account of a public encounter with him at a 2014 rally in Las Vegas. He had smelled her hair, held her shoulders, and given her "a big slow kiss on the back of my head," she wrote. For years, journalists had written about Biden's uninvited displays of affection—bumping foreheads with women (and sometimes men), rubbing noses, whispering awkwardly in people's ears. Flores, a Democrat, described feeling "anger" and "resentment." She did not consider Biden's behavior sexual—she distinguished it from the allegations of assault and misconduct that more than twenty women have made against Trump in recent years. (Trump has denied these allegations.) But, Flores said, Biden's habits showed "a lack of empathy for the women and young girls whose space he is invading." Biden, who had prided himself on his tactile approach to retail politics, responded in a statement that "not once—never—did I believe I acted inappropriately. If it is suggested I did so, I will listen respectfully. But it was never my intention."

At least six women added similar complaints. But others came forward to defend him, arguing that banishing Biden from a race against Trump, who bragged of grabbing women's genitals, would be an act of misguided absolutism. In a tweet, Biden wrote, "I've heard what these women are saying. Politics to me has always been about making connections, but I will be more mindful about respecting personal space in the future." Issues of gender flared again later in the campaign, after Tara Reade, a former Senate staffer, accused Biden of sexually assaulting her twenty-seven years earlier. She said that he pinned her to the wall in a Senate hallway, groped her, and penetrated her with his fingers. Biden emphatically denied the accusation. "It never, never happened," he said on MSNBC.

Reporters who investigated Reade's account described inconsistencies in her statements, and the potential scandal died down. Some Democrats remained unsatisfied. Biden was seeking to be the standard-bearer of a party in which rising progressives disdained not only sex abuse and harassment but also the imbalances of power that had enabled the problems to persist.

In a kickoff video, in April, Biden defined his cause as a "battle for the soul of this nation." "If we give Donald Trump eight years in the White House," he said, "he will forever and fundamentally alter the character of this nation. Who we are. And I cannot stand by and watch that happen." A few hours after Biden's announcement, as if to underscore the array of questions that he would face about his record, he was confronted with fresh headlines regarding his handling of Anita Hill's accusation of sexual harassment against Clarence Thomas in 1991. Biden had recently called Hill to express his regrets, but the call had left her unsatisfied. "I will be satisfied when I know there is real change and real accountability and real purpose," she told a reporter.

Biden began the race as the front-runner, but he seemed unfocused and out of step. During a debate, he botched an invitation to text the campaign at "30330" and instead declared, perplexingly, "Go to Joe 30330." Rather than eliciting donations, it generated a night of

Twitter memes, such as "How do you do, fellow kids?" In debates, he rarely fought back and sometimes yielded the floor with the unfortunate phrase "My time is up." Donors backed away. By February, Biden's campaign was spending less money in a month than Michael Bloomberg's spent on an average day. Kate Bedingfield, the campaign's communications director, struggled to draw attention to Biden's policy ideas. "I say the word 'achievable,' and it gets derided as 'That's not ambitious,'" she told me.

At times, Biden's disconnect looked deeper than his wobbly debate performances or his disinterest in social media. At a fund-raiser in June 2019, he teed up an anecdote he had told for years about working with the segregationist senators Herman Talmadge, of Georgia, and James Eastland, of Mississippi. "We didn't agree on much of anything," Biden said. "We got things done. We got it finished. But today you look at the other side and you're the enemy," Biden added that Eastland "never called me 'boy.' He always called me 'son.'"

One of his rivals, Senator Cory Booker, of New Jersey, issued an immediate condemnation: "You don't joke about calling Black men 'boys.'" Booker told me that what frustrated him was not that Biden had worked with segregationists. "I work with people across the aisle who have beliefs that are offensive and that defend Confederate monuments," he said. The problem was glibly boasting about it. "I did not, at that point, believe that Joe Biden understood that when people like my father were called 'boy' at work that that would be so humiliating to them," Booker said. He admires Biden, which made it worse, he told me: "It was just one of those moments that many Black people feel, where you're just, like, 'You?'" Booker was walking out of a CNN studio when Biden called to apologize. "He was willing to show me a great degree of vulnerability and to put his imperfections on the table," Booker recalled. "I've been in politics a long time—I know when I'm being worked over. I've watched him change and be willing to wrestle with this."

Biden finished a distant fourth in Iowa, and fifth in New Hampshire. The campaign was assessing how much money it would need in order to pay staffers if it shut down. Biden turned over his senior staff, promoting Dunn to the top of the campaign, and announced a promise to put the first Black woman on the Supreme Court. His polls barely budged. If he had any hope of staying in the race, it would come down to South Carolina, where Black voters make up roughly 60 percent of the Democratic Primary electorate.

No one mattered more to that process than his old friend James Clyburn, the highest-ranking African American in Congress and the godfather of South Carolina Democrats. During the civil rights movement, he and

John Lewis were among the early leaders of the Student Nonviolent Coordinating Committee. Clyburn held some distinctly progressive positions, on alleviating poverty and expanding community health centers, but he believed in hewing to the center. When he talked to young people about politics, he liked to say that as the pendulum swings from right to left and back again, it "always passes through the center." When his centrism left younger Black activists unsatisfied—as happened recently, after he tweeted "no to defunding the police"—Clyburn pointed to a display of hundreds of turtle sculptures in his office, representing a belief in slow and steady progress.

Less than a week before the primary, Clyburn and Biden were at a reception aboard the USS *Yorktown*, a retired aircraft carrier docked near Charleston. Biden had slid to second place, far behind Sanders. Clyburn ushered him into a private room and advised him, bluntly, that he needed to tighten up. "Your speeches are *senatorial*," he said. "That's not the way you win an election." He continued, "You got to look at this the way my father, the fundamentalist preacher, did on Sunday mornings. He always did it in threes. This ain't the Father, Son, and the Holy Ghost. This is about 'you, your family, and your community.'"

His urgency reflected an unapologetic pragmatism. Biden might not excite people in New York or Silicon Valley, but in South Carolina, where a white supremacist had massacred Black parishioners just after Trump announced his candidacy, the specter of four more years of Trump was graver than any policy dispute. On February 26, Clyburn supplied an emotional endorsement: "I'm fearful for my daughters and their future, and their children, and their children's future." With Biden at his side, he said, "We know Joe. But, most importantly, Joe knows us."

Biden won South Carolina by 29 points. With astonishing speed, his rivals dropped out and endorsed him. There were huge surges in turnout (up by nearly 50 percent in Texas and a hundred percent in Virginia), including many college-educated suburban independents and Republicans who had once supported candidates like Mitt Romney. On Super Tuesday, Biden won ten out of fourteen states. Sanders stayed in a while longer, but the race was effectively over.

In barely three days, Biden had gone from the edge of oblivion to victory. The turnaround was so abrupt that it stirred a sense of bafflement and suspicion, especially among young observers who had presumed his campaign was doomed. For months, even as he remained the frontrunner in polls, they had tracked his fortunes through clips of gaffes and articles about his bland assertions of centrism, which were popular on social media. Opponents on both the right and the left had promoted clips of Biden garbling his words to advance the argument that he was a senescent has-been. (In one stretch, data analysis showed that Jill Stein, the former Green Party candidate, who had more than a quarter of a million Twitter followers, succeeded in pushing #BidenCognitive Decline into a trending topic.) Even for viewers who saw none of those social media attacks, Biden had often appeared outmatched by crisper, more eloquent younger rivals, such as Pete Buttigieg, Kamala Harris, and Amy Klobuchar.

Those criticisms had never been entirely wrong. Biden, after all, *was* more than twice Buttigieg's age and had entered the campaign out of shape politically, following more than three years in private life. But, the criticisms of Biden never carried as much weight with the wider public. For people who had been listening to Biden for years, he sounded no more garbled than he ever had. He did not impress left-leaning younger members of the press corps, but they were not the cohort that crowned Democratic nominees.

In sheer political terms, he owed his success not only to help from Clyburn but also from Warren, who swiftly dispatched Bloomberg, denouncing his derogatory comments about women. Bloomberg had entered late, with a splashy pitch to centrists, but he never figured out how to manage criticism from Warren and others who were hostile to the notion of a billionaire financing his own alteration of the contest. Notwithstanding those factors, Biden adviser Ron Klain said that it was wrong to suggest that the turnaround was a fluke—"like he somehow lucked into all this." When Biden declined to savage his debate opponents, it was "strategic," Klain said. "If the only way to get the nomination was to destroy all these other people, he was going to inherit a party that wasn't going to win anyway."

Biden's years of cultivating relationships with other prominent Democrats had paid off, spectacularly. I asked Klobuchar why she endorsed Biden so fast, and she mentioned specific moments from their dealings over the years—the time he had complimented a speech during her first nervous year in the Senate; the consolation call he paid to one of her friends, after a death in the family. "There are a lot of people that have a lot of love for Joe Biden and know him well," Klobuchar told me. "We have the mission of beating Donald Trump, and I really believed that, with the power and support that was given to me, what was the best thing I could do with it? Instead of frittering it away for one more debate." She continued, "I just full-throated endorsed him. Someone said, 'Oh, did you try to negotiate things?' And I'm like, 'Are you kidding? No.'"

A less soaring telling of the primary is that Biden

benefited from fear of both Donald Trump and Bernie Sanders. Once it became clear that Biden was in a two-person race, the prospect of nominating Sanders was so unappealing to moderates—including some fellow candidates, older Black voters in places like South Carolina, and big-money donors—that they scrambled to support Biden. But Biden had also prevailed by rejecting tribalism; even as his rivals said that he was too old, too conciliatory, and too tainted by his record, he resisted responding with attack ads. His advisers believed that Biden could prevail over the "doubt in the chattering class," Kate Bedingfield, the communications chief, said. "We're not going to spend all day trying to win the latest Twitter war."

On June 1, a week after the murder of George Floyd, I walked downtown from my home in D.C. to a protest in front of the White House. After a few nights of unrest in Washington, the scene had settled into a sit-in. Protesters took turns at a bullhorn.

Among the homemade signs, I noticed a strikingly skillful painting of Floyd. It was in the hands of Kandyce Baker, a thirty-one-year-old university administrator who had come to the rally from her home, in Frederick, Maryland. "I had to do something," she told me. Baker had been especially shaken by the death of Ahmaud Arbery, who in February was tailed by three white men and shot to death while he jogged in a suburb in southern Georgia. As a marathoner and a Black woman, Baker had often run through neighborhoods where she felt unwelcome. I asked her about presidential politics. "Unfortunately, I will be voting for Biden," she said. "Bernie Sanders was my candidate." She went on, "I don't have faith that Joe Biden is going to have Black issues at the forefront. I don't feel like he's going to have millennial issues at the forefront when it comes to student loan debt. So I'm nervous."

Baker was voting, but her nervousness illuminated the risk that other young potential voters expressed misgivings about casting a vote at all. For Biden, a rejection by young Black and Latino voters could be a disaster. When Hillary Clinton ran in 2016, Black turnout declined for the first time in two decades; in some places, such as Milwaukee, the drop-off proved critical. "I'm going to vote for him because I can't have Trump in office," Baker said. "That's literally the only reason."

A few hours after I met Baker, the intersection where we talked was swarmed by police wielding batons and tear gas; they were there to sweep away protesters so that Trump could walk over from the White House and pose with a Bible in front of St. John's Episcopal Church. It was a pageant so roundly condemned that General Mark Milley, the chairman of the Joint Chiefs of Staff, publicly apologized for his presence. The incident seemed to hasten abrupt changes in the national mood. Within days, the National Football League reversed its position on kneeling during the national anthem. Booksellers across the country were swamped with orders for books about racism and Black history. Mississippi stripped the Confederate symbol from its flag.

Biden seized the moment. In a speech on July 4, he urged listeners to "rip the roots" of "systemic racism" out of American life. He joined the calls for banning police choke holds, adopting a national standard for the use of force, and narrowing "qualified immunity," the legal shield that protects public officials against federal civil rights suits. Biden's moves thrilled progressives but incensed some police. For years, he'd maintained cozy relations with the National Association of Police Organizations; now its executive director, Bill Johnson, lamented that he "used to be a stand-up guy."

Biden leapt ahead in the polls, but, as ever, he was wary of tilting too far to the left. As long as Trump was inflaming liberals by running what many perceived to be an openly racist campaign, Biden was not going to risk turning off moderate voters. Trump was already broadcasting a commercial that featured a ringing phone in a dark, empty police station. The narrator said, "If you're calling to report a rape, please press one." The ad ended with Trump's new tagline: "You won't be safe in Joe Biden's America."

Like most establishment Democrats, Biden rejected "defunding" police, a broad term for proposals that range from abolishing departments to moving money toward mental health, education, and social services. He said, however, that police should receive federal funding only if they met "basic standards of decency and honorableness," and he proposed spending $300 million to reinvigorate a decades-old idea of "community policing." David Kennedy, a professor at John Jay College of Criminal Justice, told me that he hoped Biden would adopt a newer approach to violence prevention, focusing not on communities but on individuals at the highest risk of being involved in gun violence. Such a program, applied nationally, "could cut in half the gun violence that devastates America's minority communities, without doing the damage of traditional policing," Kennedy said.

When I spoke with Biden about the prospects for real change—to incarceration, policing, and entrenched racism—he offered an analogy to the civil rights era, and the iconically cruel police boss of Birmingham. "When I was a kid in high school, Bull Connor sics his dogs on those elderly Black women going to church in their Sunday dress, and on little kids, with fire hoses, literally ripping their skin off," he said. "He thought he was driving a wooden stake into the heart of the civil rights movement." Instead, images of the violence consolidated support behind Martin Luther King Jr., and forced white leaders in Washington to take steps that led to the Voting Rights Act of 1965. In Biden's telling, white people in America were now experiencing a similar awakening, prompted by the horrific images of police violence captured by cell phones. Lifting his phone from the arm of the chair, he said, "This phone has changed a lot of things. Watching Floyd's face pinned against that curb and his nose being crushed, I mean, the vividness of it was, like, 'Holy God. That still happens today?'"

He extended that image, of a dawning awareness, to the Covid-19 crisis. "People who've been able to shelter in place realized the only way I can get in and out of the drugstore is if someone stacks that shelf. Or the grocery store. Or the person delivering the mail. Or the person who is going to make sure that the food gets to me. The first responder. And they look out there, and they're *seeing* it." And as the virus spread, the impact was becoming more personal. "They *know* somebody who has lost a life. They know somebody who has had Covid-19. Because, for the first two months, it was like, 'Well, yeah, it's terrible but I don't *know* anybody.'"

Biden said that the turmoil of 2020 had dismantled a myth deeply embedded in his consciousness. For years, he'd been telling a parable about the morning of Obama's Inauguration: "I called my two sons and my daughter up, and I said, 'Guys, don't tell me things can't change.'" Hunching forward in his seat, he told me that Trump had exposed the flaw in that parable. "I'm embarrassed to say, I thought you could defeat hate. You can't. It only hides," he said. "It crawls under the rocks, and, when given oxygen by any person in authority, it comes roaring back out. And what I realized is, the words of a president, even a lousy president, matter. They can take you to war, they can bring peace, they can make the market rise, they can make it fall. But they can also give hate oxygen."

In the usual course of a presidential campaign, a Democrat leans left during the primary and then marches right in the general election. Biden went the opposite direction. Exit polls had revealed a stark warning: even in states where he prevailed, many voters preferred the more ambitious plans, from Sanders and Warren, on issues like the economy and health care.

Within weeks, Biden had picked up Warren's plan to ease student debt and overhaul the bankruptcy system—

which entailed repealing parts of a law he had helped pass. He embraced a limited version of Sanders's plan for tuition-free college, and dropped his opposition to federal funding for abortions. Almost precisely a year after assuring skittish voters that "nothing would fundamentally change," Biden said that America was due for "some revolutionary institutional changes."

Once it became clear that Biden would secure the nomination, Sanders endorsed him—moving far more quickly than he had in 2016. "I have a better relationship with Joe Biden than I had with Hillary Clinton," Sanders explained, candidly. To unify their platforms, Biden and Sanders set up task forces on criminal justice, economics, education, health care, immigration, and climate change. The task forces were a crucial test of whether the left and center factions of the party could get along. Both sides were wary. Biden told me, "I had to be sure that Bernie was serious, that he wasn't going to make this an ideological jihad. I said, 'Bernie, if you want these set up in order for me to insist that I be for Medicare for All . . . this is not where it's going to go.' But I said, 'I'm open, I hear you, I'm ready to listen.'"

Biden recruited Ocasio-Cortez to chair the climate task force, alongside former secretary of state John Kerry. Members included Varshini Prakash, of the Sunrise Movement, the youth-led climate-action group, which during the primary had graded Biden's climate plan an F. At the first meeting, Kerry asked Prakash to lead off. The Sanders contingent wanted all-clean electricity by 2030; they were happy to settle for 2035. The biggest unresolved point of contention was fracking. Biden opposes new oil-and-gas development on federal lands and waters, but, unlike Sanders, he has not called for a total ban on fracking. "It's not like I walked out of there with Bernie's Green New Deal in hand, and I did not expect to," Prakash said. "But it was a lot more collaborative, actually, than I was anticipating."

Sean McElwee, an influential activist who cofounded the nonprofit think tank Data for Progress, criticized Biden fiercely at the outset of the campaign. But by July, his view had changed. "I think a lot of people who just shit on the Democratic Party haven't spent a lot of time talking to mainstream actors within the Democratic Party ecosystem," he told me. "The reality is, that ecosystem is very liberal." He continued, "I think people should just take a step back and look at what Biden has done. AOC is someone I like a lot. She said that she wouldn't vote for him in the primary, and that in a different country she would be in a different party from him. And he could have responded to that by being, like, 'Fuck you.' But instead he responded to that by being, like, 'How about you come in and write my climate policy?'"

• • •

On a weekday afternoon in late July, Biden was at a pre-school in New Castle, Delaware, preparing to talk about economics. Schools had been closed for months, because of the virus; on the playground, the swings were coiled out of reach. Inside, Biden was holding a simulacrum of a campaign event that resembled a scene from an avant-garde play: no crowds, no rope lines, just a scattering of reporters, each of us masked and marooned in a white cardboard ring. The PA system was playing Alicia Keys and Beyoncé to a silent, huddled assemblage.

The economic shutdown had produced what Jerome Powell, the chairman of the Federal Reserve, called a "level of pain that is hard to capture in words." Forty per-cent of the low-income Americans who had jobs in Feb-ruary lost them in March and early April. Twelve years after the financial crisis, the virus had again exploded corporate America's mythology of self-reliance. Some of the largest payments in a congressional rescue package intended for small businesses went instead to the finan-cial sector. Millions of dollars in emergency cash went to "family offices," the personal investment companies that manage fortunes for hedge fund billionaires and other wealthy individuals.

Biden stepped to the lectern to announce a $775 billion investment in the caregiving economy, providing funds for universal preschool, in-home care for the elderly, and paid family leave, of the sort that is routine in other developed nations. The plan clearly targeted the needs of Americans who strain to balance work with caring for children and, often, aging parents. "I was a single parent for five years," Biden told the reporters. "Even though I had a lot more support than a lot of people going through tough times today, it was hard." The plan, he said, was "a moral and economic imperative." It would be funded partly by rolling back Trump-era tax breaks for real estate investors. Ai-jen Poo, who leads the National Domestic Workers Alliance, tweeted that Biden's proposal marked the first time in twenty years that a presidential candidate had made "investments in the care economy a core strategy in their economic agenda. Not a side issue, an add-on, or a special interest." A Trump campaign spokesman responded to the proposal by saying that it would "remake America with socialist policies."

The caregiving plan was the latest in a series of speeches in which Biden had called for sweeping economic changes. He planned to spend $700 billion on American products and research, to create jobs around electric cars, artificial intelligence, and other technologies, without the tariffs and the perceived xenophobia of Trump's "America First" policy. He had announced a $2 trillion clean energy and infrastructure plan that would eliminate carbon emissions from power plants by 2035.

For all of Biden's Rooseveltian zeal, it was unclear how far he would go on the explosive issues of wealth, taxes, and corporate exploitation. At a fund-raiser in July, hosted by investors and executives, Biden said, "Corporate America has to change its ways." Then he added a comment that inflamed progressives: "It's not going to require legislation. I'm not proposing any." When we spoke, I asked what he meant. No legislation? "That is really shorthand," Biden said. As he explained it, America's corporate establishment has acknowledged the need for fundamental changes. He cited the Business Roundtable, a group of corporate CEOs, which last year announced a shift away from the dominant focus on shareholder value. He said, "All those people understood that they are eating their own seed corn."

Nevertheless, he told me that he would push for legislation: a measure, proposed by Warren, to forbid companies to use excess revenues to purchase their own stock, rather than to invest in wage increases or in research. "What they have to understand is they have a responsibility," he said. "As Barack had said when we were running, 'You didn't build this alone.' That $20 million highway interchange—we put in for you. It helps everybody." He went on, "I've been talking with a bunch of my economists, saying, 'What are the types of legislation that require greater corporate responsibility?' That has to occur."

I sensed that Biden was straining to say as little as possible about his economic vision, which seemed to be less a matter of tactical evasion than of ideological uncertainty. He was confronting a moment of almost impossible political and economic complexity—the nominee of a party gradually marching left, which was desperate to win over moderates and Republicans who were terrified of that march to the left. Biden was more than sentimentally attached to the working class, and he was embracing some leftist technocratic fixes that would help it. But he gave no indication that he was preparing for a bitter, costly fight to overturn the primacy of the corporate establishment. As Maurice Mitchell, of the Working Families Party, put it, "We've already put trillions of dollars into the economy with bailout after bailout. Are we propping up systems that have brought us here?"

In ways that nobody could have predicted, the 2020 campaign was shaping up as a referendum not only on Trump's moral fitness, but on the architecture of American power—a system that Biden had helped develop and refine over half a century in public life. As the race entered its final months, the narrow goal of replacing Trump no longer sufficed. Biden was awakening to the full scale of an emergency even larger than he had imagined.

CHAPTER 8

Planning a Presidency

"People say to me, 'Well, what are you going to do if you get elected?'" Biden said, throwing his hands out to his sides. He answered his own question: "It depends on what the hell I'm left with. Not a joke. I'm not being a wise guy. Things could get a lot worse," he added.

As fall arrived, the pandemic continued to spread relentlessly. The United States remained the world's worst performer, with more than six million cases, and a pace of infection that had barely subsided. Daily death counts in August had been more than double the average for early July. Any vaccine remained months away.

Under the circumstances, his campaign was preparing a transition unlike others, beginning with the prospect of a socially distanced Inauguration. ("You don't have to have a crowd," Biden said.) Using executive action, Biden could, almost immediately, take steps to rejoin the World

Health Organization and the Paris Climate Agreement, and remove Trump's immigration restrictions on Muslim countries.

Meanwhile, his strategists were developing an unusually rapid timeline for legislation. "The strategy is: go fast, be bold," Jake Sullivan, a top policy adviser, told me. "Don't fall into the trap of thinking we have to line things up in a sequence according to a traditional political calculus, because these are anything but traditional times." Under normal circumstances, a president rushes to make legislative achievements in the first two years, while there is still the glow of victory and a backlash has not yet shifted control of Congress. "He's not thinking on a two-year time frame, he's thinking on a first-few-months time frame," Sullivan said.

For all of Biden's odes to FDR, their political environments had scarcely little in common; modern Washington is far more oppositional and antagonistic than in Roosevelt's day, which could thwart any attempt to make sweeping change on health care, climate change, and other issues. To avoid that, Biden and his advisers mapped out strategies ranging from comity and charm to "scorched earth," as one of Biden's strategists put it to me.

Their approach hinged on which party won a majority of seats in Congress. If Republicans retained control of the Senate, Biden suspected he could attract a few moderate Republicans to join him and Democrats on deals for popular items such as infrastructure investment. Though progressives lampooned that notion as naive, Biden and his advisers maintained that they would be proven right, as they had been in the primary. "Conventional wisdom was, one, Biden wouldn't win. Everyone who votes is young and liberal, and he's old and ancient," an aide told me. "Well, Biden managed to unify this party faster than we thought was even possible."

No matter which party controlled Congress, Biden would likely prioritize certain progressive goals—such as raising the minimum wage, and taking drastic steps to address climate change—while sidestepping more polarizing proposals, such as decriminalizing the border, or extending free Medicare to undocumented immigrants.

Some analysts believed that Biden's reputation as a centrist could make it easier for him to achieve changes that might seem more threatening coming from a doctrinaire progressive. In research by Sean McElwee, the progressive pollster, swing voters were more likely to support climate change action if it was framed as a way to create good jobs and to bring down energy costs, rather than as a moral obligation to future generations.

In that light, members of Biden's circle compared him to Lyndon Johnson, who used his decades of legislative experience in the House and the Senate to achieve more liberal gains than Kennedy, the symbol of dynamism and generational change. "LBJ might not have been the wokest, coolest, hippest Democrat, but he's the person who got the most actual progressive social justice legislation done since FDR," Ron Klain, the Biden adviser, said. "It was because of two things. He brought in a bunch of Democrats with him in 1964, so he had a good strong majority, and he knew how to make the Senate work."

Mike Donilon, who has advised Biden on and off for thirty years, told me Biden rejects the usual argument that the canyon between Republicans and Democrats has widened to the point that even basic negotiation is impossible: "While it may feel or seem like we're in separate camps, that's not how he would approach the presidency. You try to work with the other side. You actually try to listen. You don't start out by saying, 'I don't trust this person. I've got nothing in common with them.'" Donilon said Biden believes people in Washington often negotiate in precisely the wrong way: "Everyone immediately goes to the bottom-line absolute toughest moment in the negotiation. They're, like, 'We've got to solve this before we solve anything else.' So you don't solve that— and you don't solve anything else." He said, "It doesn't mean we compromise on principles, but you've got to at least see them." Donilon knows people think that is naive. "Maybe he'll hit a stone wall, although I actually think the desire in the country for it"—for signs of comity and compromise—"is going to be quite high," he said. "Democrats said for a long time with Biden, 'You're living in another world. It doesn't exist anymore.' I kind of feel the country really is going to be at the moment where it wants to embrace it."

Some of Biden's and Donilon's talk of moderation reflected a certain pre-election prudence—a need to attract moderates and disaffected Republicans. The harsher reality was that even if Democrats gained three seats in the Senate, affording them control of both houses of Congress, they might still need to resort to brute political force. Democrats, for instance, could use a budget rule called "reconciliation" to pass laws with a simple Senate majority, a tactic that Trump and congressional Republicans used to achieve their 2017 tax overhaul. In a more dramatic step, many frustrated Democrats are eager to scrap the filibuster, a Senate tradition that prevents progress on bills by forcing one side to assemble a supermajority of sixty votes. Even establishment Democrats were desperate for change; Obama, in July 2020, threw his voice behind the calls for abolition, arguing that it would allow Democrats to make bold changes to election rules, including automatically registering Americans to vote, establishing Election Day as a federal holiday, giving equal representation to citizens of Washington, D.C., and Puerto Rico, and ending partisan gerrymandering.

When I spoke to Obama in July, he emphasized his belief that Democrats could no longer afford to make fruitless attempts at bipartisanship: "One of the things that I think all of us who believe in democracy have had to contend with is the growing recognition that the Republican Party made a decision to change how they operated in a way that makes it very difficult for democracy to function. And, part of the cynicism of that is their recognition that if democracy's not working, if there's gridlock and bitter partisanship and division, that discourages and tamps down our voters more than theirs. And they don't necessarily mind if government comes to a standstill."

Biden, notably, was more conservative. He stopped short of endorsing Obama's call for abolishing the filibuster— the greatest point of tactical disagreement between them. Democrats, he said cautiously, should "take a look at" at eliminating or modifying the filibuster, but only if Republicans proved to be "obstreperous." When Justice Ruth Bader Ginsburg died, in September, the prospect of a partisan rapprochement seemed to recede even further.

Among the unusually delicate challenges Biden would face upon arrival in the White House would be the matter of handling Donald Trump himself. Private citizen Trump would pose challenges both political and legal. Even before the election, he told his supporters that he could only lose if it was "rigged"; Democrats, strategizing about the near future, considered the prospect that Trump would incite unrest. Biden's aides had no choice but to discuss scenarios once confined to farce: "People throw around the idea that, well, he's just going to chain himself to the bed in the Lincoln bedroom and not go," one of Biden's top aides told me. In practice, they expected the broad machinery of the state to reject any effort to squat in the West Wing. "On January 20th, constitutionally, the next president takes power, and then has all of the tools of government at their disposal," the aide said, a pointed reference to the military and police. In a more likely challenge, how would a Biden administration respond to pressure of a different kind: the demand—already building before Election Day—to hold his predecessor's administration accountable for corruption, negligence, and mismanagement?

Kevin Kruse, a Princeton historian, called on Biden to undertake an investigation into the administration's handling of the pandemic, modeled on the Pecora Commission, a Senate inquiry into the causes of the crash of 1929. Named for the lead investigator, Ferdinand Pecora, the probe exposed vast corruption atop some of

America's most respected institutions, where bankers had awarded themselves hidden bonuses and doled out stocks at below-market prices to secret lists of elite clients. The revelations generated public support for sweeping economic and political reforms under Roosevelt's New Deal, including creation of the Securities and Exchange Commission. Kruse said, "There is precedent here. Traditionally, when something goes horribly wrong, especially when thousands of Americans die, there would be a major inquiry, like the 9-11 Commission."

Kruse hoped a Covid-19 commission would also lead to a broader investigation of what he saw as Trump-era corruption and negligence. "That's going to be a harder sell, politically, because some will surely characterize an effort at accountability as little more than political payback." The Obama administration did not prosecute major purveyors of toxic loans or derivatives, or torturers directed by the CIA, largely because Obama preferred, as he said at the time, to "look forward as opposed to looking backwards." Kruse calls that a mistake: "Every time we do that, every time we mistake basic accountability for baseless vindictiveness, we invariably pay a price for it later on. When wrongdoers who should be held accountable skate, they often return to roles of public importance later on, and they're emboldened because they know they got away with it once before," he said. "If you don't hold people accountable, it only undermines faith in our institutions, because they can say, quite rightly, 'Well, I went to prison for something small. These people did much worse but they got away with it.'"

Biden dismissed suggestions that he could prosecute specific individuals—"That will be for the professionals in the Justice Department"—but, after Trump sidelined the inspector general who had been assigned to oversee the pandemic response, Biden pledged to appoint an inspector general who could probe the $2.2 trillion stimulus program passed by Congress in March. "Any dollar taken corruptly, we will find it, we will come get it and we will punish the wrongdoers," he said. That investigator could refer potential criminal activity to the Justice Department in what Biden called a warning "to anyone who participates in the corrupt giveaways of President Trump and his administration."

When I spoke to Pete Buttigieg about seeking accountability for Trump, he argued that young Americans are less inclined to see a turning of the page—such as Gerald Ford's 1974 pardon of his predecessor, Richard Nixon—as a noble act of renewal. "I think the commission idea is really interesting. Whatever happens has to be set up in a way that makes it possible for the Republican Party to move on from Trumpism and come to terms with how it got captured by it. It can't just be a partisan process of victor's justice. This has to be about national healing and values and norms."

The criticism that the Obama administration did not do enough to hold its predecessors accountable was surprisingly popular even among some of the officials involved at the time. One of Obama's aides told me, "The lesson of the early Obama years is that there's nothing really gained from not holding more people accountable. There need not be politically motivated prosecutions of course, but if there is a reason for the rule of law to hold people accountable, then that should be allowed to proceed. We earned no points, from either the Republicans or the business community, for not pursuing prosecutions, and likely lost an opportunity to affix the blame where it should have rested for the economic and national security disasters Obama inherited."

In the first hundred days of a Biden administration, while trying to establish his agenda, he would not only be contending with opponents on the right; he would be at least as likely to face resistance within his own party. In August, the Sunrise Movement, the climate change group, addressed a tweet to "Establishment Democrats" and promised to be a persistent source of criticism even after Trump's departure: "Biden is just a tool to kick Trump out of the White House. Get ready for four years of hell from a generation of angry young people." To understand what methods he might employ to bind the disparate factions of his party, from centrists to the Ocasio-Cortez wing, I met with Michael Kazin, a historian and the coeditor of the leftist quarterly *Dissent*, for a socially distanced interview at a Washington, D.C., park. We took opposite ends of a picnic table, like spies in a Cold War novel.

"Obama raised people's expectations," Kazin told me. "People on the left—to use this too-aggregated term— would say, 'We like what he promised to do, but he didn't follow through.' The question was how much was his fault, how much was structural impediments, and how much was the timing and what he had to do to save the economy." Kazin went on, "Some of it is because he believed in bipartisanship. He thought too much of his own abilities, I think, to persuade people on the basis of his personality and his rhetoric."

Kazin made a case, to my surprise, that young progressives would support elements of Biden's agenda more readily than their most fiery rhetoric suggests. "A lot of people on the left, and young left especially, think the Democratic Party has to be torn up, root and branch, and run by AOC and people like her. But, strategically, they realize that's not where people are now," he said. "They're working on electing left-wing Democrats who will try to get Medicare for All, free college, better public housing, police reform, or even defunding. These are all necessary radical reforms, but they're still reforms." Kazin cited a recent article in *Dissent* calling for mandatory voting, akin to laws in Australia. "That's not going to happen," he added, "but if it did that would be amazing." Exploring those ideas is part of the work of loyal opposition. "Look, we're a radical magazine. We have to talk about things like that. I don't think we're going to defund the police either, but I'm in favor of people talking about it."

To keep the left in a coalition, Kazin said, Biden will need to follow through on plans to double the minimum wage and make it easier to form unions. "That probably won't happen all at once. But unions, even those that supported Bernie, are now mostly behind him because they realize this could be really good," Kazin said. "Biden realizes something which Obama somehow didn't understand, that unions are a necessary part of the Democratic base. If you have more union members, Democrats will do better. You can see that among white voters: white union voters voted for Clinton, whereas white nonunion voters voted overwhelmingly for Trump. It's just a huge difference." Most of all, Kazin said, if Biden wants to live up to a Rooseveltian promise, he will need to focus on restoring the faith of Americans, of any political stripe, that government can address their needs. "Government worked in the 1930s. Government worked during World War II. That's why people believed, and that's why they kept electing either liberals or moderate Republicans," he said. These days, the confidence has been lost. "You've got to convince people that government can actually do what it says it'll do. People on the left just assume, 'Medicare for All, people will love it!' Well, yeah. If it works."

Obama endorsed that view. He predicted that progressives would accept some flexibility if it produces results. "I don't think it is the actual items on the policy checklist that they're going to be looking for," he said. "What they're going to want to see is, Show us that you can make the machinery of government work to reflect what we believe in and what we care about. Show us that if the majority of Americans support doing something about climate change, that you can actually get something done, and it doesn't just get ground down to nothing by the time it gets through the U.S. Senate or the U.S. House."

One method by which Biden could build support from the left would be by hiring progressives to influential jobs in his administration. A senior Sanders adviser told me, "Frankly, if you look at the Obama years, there wasn't a hell of a lot of progressive challenge internally. Where was the internal voice saying 'Hey, you're just compromising too much. You've got to go fight these bastards'?" In a Biden administration, he continued, "It could be in the cabinet. It could be personnel around him. If he represents one wing of the Democratic Party in a defined manner—the establishment—then it's really incumbent on those who have power to say, 'Okay, what efforts do you want to make to reach out to those who lost?'"

Biden made some gestures in that direction. For years, he had relied on a small clutch of aides, including Donilon, Klain, and Kaufman—a lineup that *Politico Magazine* described last year as "a lot like Biden: old and white and with long experience in Democratic Party battles of a bygone era." But the portrait ignored the likes of Symone Sanders, a thirty-year-old former Bernie Sanders aide who was among the most influential Black advisers in Biden's campaign. Biden recognized that meeting the needs of the country would require a radical expansion of the people and the experiences represented around him. "I think it's really important—really, really important— that my administration look like the country," he told me. He hoped to be remembered, he said, as someone who "brought along an awful lot of really talented people who would not otherwise have the chance or the exposure."

I was often struck that moderate Democrats tended

to describe the ideological gulf in the party as a manageable level of disagreement. When I suggested to Klobuchar, the moderate Democrat from Minnesota, that Biden might have trouble maintaining support from the left, she said, "I don't buy it." The real gulf was between people who support or oppose Trump. "The gulf within our own party is not nearly as huge," she said. "Look at the police reform bill in the House and the Senate; a bunch of moderates in the House and from rural areas supported that bill."

For all of the rhetoric coming out of the Sunrise Movement's twitter account, Prakash, one of the group's founders, told me that it saw a Biden presidency as an opportunity. "We have to get this guy elected president, and move from the realm of policy to power," she said. "Progressive things have happened in this country under pretty moderate presidents, in the right time and the right place. We created the EPA under Nixon! We created the interstate highway system under Eisenhower." She laughed. "The key is not to become either complacent or righteous," she said. "Find a strong place in the middle there."

Over the summer, as Trump sank in the polls, Biden reached numbers unmatched by any challenger to an incumbent since the advent of modern polling. Even after Trump used the White House as a backdrop for convention events, he still failed to get the usual bounce in his polls. Biden often said he was seeking to "unify the nation." But what would that actually mean? Was the pursuit of unity a recipe for paralysis?

The prospect of unity had helped lift Obama into the White House. But the valence of the concept had changed. "The Obama electorate, that innocent cohort of Americans, has grown up," Mitchell, of the Working Families Party, told me. "They're more cynical. They're hardened. They ask more questions, they want more data. People want to understand: 'What are the policy details?' People go online, read plans and scrutinize them. So, Biden needs to articulate, 'If we flip the Senate, these other things will happen. And this is what my cabinet will look like, and these are the Trump-era decisions that we will reverse.' You can't just speak in broad prose."

When I asked Obama what he expected to unfold, he was spending part of the summer at his house on Martha's Vineyard, laboring over his presidential memoir. He endorsed Biden soon after Sanders dropped out, and had played a surgical public role in the campaign— appearing alongside the candidate in a video conversation and at a fund-raiser. He and Biden spoke frequently by phone, though they didn't draw much attention to those exchanges. Trump, after all, would have loved to portray a Biden administration as a covert restoration of the Obama years. Obama had recently garnered attention for a rousing oration at the funeral for John Lewis reminding beleaguered Democrats of a largely forgotten era of optimism.

I asked him about young people who were dismayed that the Democratic establishment had not achieved greater progress. He raised the example of health care. "Joe and I were both painfully aware of some of the constraints and limitations," he said. "But it's what we could get done then, and twenty-plus million people got health insurance. Missouri just expanded Medicaid, so maybe that's several hundred thousand more. And now you have an opportunity to make it that much better. So I think one response to the younger generation is, Yes, you should push harder! Because that's how progress happens."

Obama is touchy about suggestions that his administration was too willing to compromise. "My legislative agenda, Joe's legislative agenda, was at least as bold and aggressive as many of the young people's agendas right now," he said. "If you asked Joe and I what regrets we might have, or what lessons we learned from my administration, it's not that we were insufficiently bold in what we proposed. It's that we continued to believe in the capacity of Republicans in Congress to play by the rules, and to be willing to negotiate and compromise."

When Obama ran for reelection, in 2012, he hoped that a victory would lead to a more amenable Congress. "The fever may break," he said at the time, "because there's a tradition in the Republican Party of more common sense than that." That hope was long gone. "When I speak to young people, I say to them, Look, our climate proposals were very aggressive—we just couldn't get them passed," he told me. "And the reason we couldn't get them passed was not because lobbyists and corporate donors were whispering in our ears! The reason we couldn't pass them was because we didn't have sixty votes in the Senate. And the same is true for getting a public option on health care, and getting immigration reform passed." Obama went on, "Through its actions, the Republican Party has discredited the old-style negotiations and compromises that existed in Congress when Joe first came in. And it's probably taken him a little time to let go of that, because I think he has experience of being able to get stuff done. And I think it's been painful for him, to see what's happened to institutions like the Senate."

Biden often argued that America "cannot function without generating consensus." But, when he conjured the image of congressional harmony, many younger Americans thought that he sounded deluded—or, worse, unwilling to join difficult fights. He was mocked in 2019 for suggesting that members of Congress would undergo an "epiphany" after Trump was gone. To his mind, though, the prospects for bipartisanship hinged on the margin of victory. "If we win, and we pick up five or six Senate seats, I think there *will* be an epiphany," he told me, "because all you need then is three, or four, or five Republicans who have seen the light a little bit." He went on, "I don't think you can underestimate the impact of Trump not being there. The vindictiveness, the pettiness, the willingness to, at his own expense, go after people with vendettas, like you saw with Sessions"—Jeff Sessions, the former attorney general, whom Trump had helped torpedo in the recent Alabama primary.

One senior Obama administration official I spoke to over the summer worried that Biden's optimism could be costly: "Does he see his role as someone who can bring in the Never Trumpers and build some bipartisan consensus? I know from experience that's a trap. We walked right into it. Your people lose faith, the Republicans never give you credit, you waste a lot of time—and you end up with the Tea Party."

In August, facing one of the most revealing tests of his campaign, Biden made a telling choice: he picked Kamala Harris, the junior senator from California, as his running mate. For the moment, he was championing racial and ethnic diversity over ideological diversity. She would be the first Black person, the first South Asian, and the first woman to serve as vice president. Like Biden, she was never the choice of progressives. Though she had one of the Senate's most liberal voting records, progressives were uncomfortable with many of her choices as San Francisco's district attorney and as California's attorney general, when she hesitated to make some police reforms and aggressively prosecuted truancy.

At Biden's side for the announcement, Harris showed a ready appetite for the fray, saying of Trump's economy, "Like everything else he inherited, he ran it straight into the ground," and hammering him for the fact that "an American dies of Covid-19 every eighty seconds." Trump and his surrogates struggled to agree on a mode of attack; they mocked Harris's voice and her name, and, in an email to supporters, called her "the meanest, most horrible, most disrespectful, MOST LIBERAL of anyone in the U.S. Senate."

After the announcement, I called Kandyce Baker, the university administrator I met at a rally, who had described herself as "unfortunately" supporting Biden. Baker was pleased to have a Black woman on the ticket but wary of the political calculations. "I'm all for candidates changing their position or recognizing, like, 'Hey, that was 2015, and now I have more information.' But I need Kamala to explain what happened," Baker said. "It's not enough to just say you've evolved."

When Harris spoke at the Democratic National Convention, in late August, she offered more encouragement than explanations. "I'm so inspired by a new generation," she said. "You are pushing us to realize the ideals of our nation." Harris was beginning to stake out a role in a Biden administration. She was unlikely to be the liaison to Congress that Biden had been for Obama, because Biden would do that himself. Instead, she showed potential to be a public bridge to younger, more diverse constituencies, and a forceful voice of the administration's values in rebuttal to Trumpism, beginning with an upcoming debate against Vice President Mike Pence. Biden prided himself on having been a loyal vice president, and Harris would need to manage her instant new status as the party's heir apparent, without alienating her boss.

The convention, like so many things these days, was confined to screens, but the constraints only accentuated the sense of personal urgency. Obama presented a stirring appeal to Americans, especially the young, to reject cynicism and apathy. "That's how a democracy withers until it's no democracy at all, and we cannot let that happen," he said. In his telling, individualism conveyed responsibility, not license. "Do not let them take away your power," he warned.

It was all a prelude to Biden's sobering case for moral decency, for reasonableness, for mourning what he called this "season of darkness." In a speech that did not mention Trump by name, Biden argued that Americans are not captive to the failures of the past and the present. "I will draw on the best of us, not the worst," he declared, and quoted Ella Baker, the icon of civil rights, who said, "Give people light and they will find a way."

One after another, ordinary people attested to enduring hardship. Kristin Urquiza, a thirty-nine-year-old from Arizona, told the story of her father, Mark Anthony Urquiza, who had voted for Trump, believed his assurances about the pandemic, and, she said, "died alone, in the ICU, with a nurse holding his hand." Brayden Harrington, a thirteen-year-old from New Hampshire, gave credit to Biden for telling him that they belonged to "the same club—we stutter." The official roll call, usually a banal ritual on the convention floor, was reborn as a video parade, surveying America's diversity and vastness, from the Caribbean to the Dakotas and Alaska. The effect was kitschy and comforting and exhilarating, befitting an era in which Americans are waking to an unsettling conviction: a politician may give us light, or at least not obscure it, but we must find the way.

• • •

For all the puzzles over policy and tactics that awaited a potential Biden presidency—China, climate change, AI, not to mention the crises in the foreground—its essential character seemed likely to emerge from a deeper set of decisions. His prescriptions for America's troubles would be informed by two divergent strands of his biography: the myths that undergird the politics of responsibility, and his own encounters with misfortune. In *The Tyranny of Merit*, Harvard political philosopher Michael Sandel wrote, "Even as inequality has widened to vast proportions, the public culture has reinforced the notion that we are responsible for our fate and deserve what we get. . . . If we succeed, it is thanks to our own doing, and if we fail, we have no one to blame but ourselves." In the age of pandemic and systemic injustice, Sandel argued, "a lively sense of the contingency of our lot conduces to a certain humility: 'There, but for the grace of God, or the accident of birth, or the mystery of fate, go I.'"

Biden, ever the weathervane, was betting that America wanted a different politics. He understood what went on in the minds of Congress members—the balancing, the hedging, the triangulation—and he believed that at least a few of them were ready to cooperate with him. But his image of unity put even greater weight on a force beyond the mechanics of Washington: the prospect of making people feel as if someone in the capital was listening.

Every day during the uniquely strange presidential campaign of 2020, Biden's aides tried to get him on the phone with a regular person. One afternoon in the spring, he was patched through to Mohammad Qazzaz, in Dearborn, Michigan. Three weeks earlier, Qazzaz, who ran a coffee-roasting business, had tested positive for Covid-19. When Biden called, he was quarantined in his house, trying to protect his wife and two children.

Qazzaz, who recorded the call and played it for me, told Biden that his daughter, who was two, did not understand why he would not come out of his bedroom: "She keeps telling me, 'Baba, open the door! Open the door.'" As he described his situation, his voice broke, and he tried to steady himself. "I'm sorry, Mr. Vice President," he said.

"Don't be sorry," Biden said. "I think your emotional state is totally justified. And, as my mom would say, you have to get it out."

Biden told Qazzaz that he, too, once had children too small to understand a crisis unfolding around them. "Nothing is the same, but I have some sense of what you're going through," Biden said. He suggested that Qazzaz play a simple game with his daughter through the door, asking her to guess a number or a color. "Tell her stories about what it's going to be like when Daddy gets better," he said. They talked for a while about Qazzaz's father, who emigrated from Jerusalem. "Look, you're going to get through this," Biden said. "We are the nation we are because we're a nation of immigrants." The call was supposed to last five minutes; they talked for twenty-two.

Listening to Qazzaz's call put me in mind of Franklin Roosevelt's famous line: "The presidency is not merely an administrative office. . . . It is pre-eminently a place of moral leadership." Joe Biden's life was replete with mistakes and regrets and staggering personal loss. And, if he came to the presidency, he was unlikely to supply much of the exalted rhetoric that reaches into a nation's soul. But, for a people in mourning, he might offer something like solace, a language of healing.

Acknowledgments

Most of this writing originated in *The New Yorker*, where I am particularly grateful to my colleagues, current and former. My first profile of Biden was edited by the esteemed John Bennet. Shorter installments were improved by Virginia Cannon, Amy Davidson Sorkin, and Carla Blumenkranz. When I returned to the subject at length during the 2020 campaign, I had the good fortune to be edited by Nick Trautwein, who is blessed with the candor and precision of a surgeon. I am especially indebted to Deirdre Foley-Mendelssohn, Dorothy Wickenden, and David Remnick, who sustain the magazine's culture of fairness, progress, and productive obsession.

At various points, this work benefited from the essential work of fact-checking and other editorial support by Madeleine Baverstam, James Haynes, Ethan Jewell, Ruth Margalit, Teresa Mathew, Betsy Morais, Matthew Silberman, Hélène Werner, and Hannah Wilentz.

This book would not have happened without the brilliance of my friend and agent Jennifer Joel. Special

ACKNOWLEDGMENTS

thanks to Jonathan Karp, who has encouraged my work for many years, long before he moved some planets to publish this volume. At Scribner, Nan Graham greeted this idea with gracious urgency and editor Colin Harrison became a stalwart partner on every page. Thanks, as well, to Sarah Goldberg, Mark LaFlaur, and Brian Belfiglio.

My greatest debt, always, is at home: To my wife, Sarabeth, whose immunity to cynicism informs my every word on politics; and to Oliver and Rose, who remind us exactly why these matters matter.

Note on Sources

This book is adapted from an occasional series of articles published by *The New Yorker*, between 2011 and 2020. Biden has spent much of his life telling people, "You're either on the way up or you're on the way down." The first time I met him—in April 2014—he was in midair, professionally and literally, aboard Air Force Two over Eastern Europe, in the doldrums of his second term as vice president. Washington was paralyzed by partisan rancor, Obama's approval rating was ailing, and it was too early for Biden to begin overt discussions of running for president. Over the years, I conducted four interviews with Biden, most recently in July 2020. Along the way, I interviewed more than a hundred people in his political orbit, including Obama on two occasions, members of Biden's family and longtime aides, as well as opponents and associates in Washington, Delaware, and elsewhere.

Biden became an area of accidental expertise. I had initially gravitated to him as a subject because he was involved in foreign affairs, and I had spent a decade as a correspondent overseas. But, up close, I came to see in him a more rewarding well of insight into American political culture, because of the span of his experience, the range of his emotional intensity, and his difficulty in disguising his thinking with the full depth of horseshit that adorns many encounters in Washington journalism. Biden spins, of course, but not quite as smoothly as others do.

In addition to my interviews, I benefited from the work of

a range of scholars and journalists, who have documented his career and its context. The notes below are not intended to be exhaustive; they are, I hope, a roadmap to some especially valuable sources.

PROLOGUE

The account of Biden's aneurysms, and his recovery, is drawn from interviews with him and his family members. As with most major episodes in his life, I was also informed by valuable details in his memoirs, *Promises to Keep* (2007) and *Promise Me, Dad: A Year of Hope, Hardship, and Purpose* (2017). Other insights on his medical crisis appear in *What It Takes: The Way to the White House*, by the late Richard Ben Cramer, the unrivaled account of Biden's run for president in 1987.

Biden's comment to a minister in a private meeting is drawn from my interview with a firsthand witness.

CHAPTER 1: ANNUS HORRIBILIS

James Comey's characterization appeared in his memoir, *A Higher Loyalty: Truth, Lies, and Leadership* (New York: Flatiron Books, 2018).

I am grateful to Patrick Fisher for his insights on the political effects of the millennial wave, which appear in multiple publications, including "Generational Cycles in American Politics, 1952–2016," *Society* 57 (2020): 22–29.

For observations on the evolution of young left, I benefited from an in-depth essay by John Judis, "A Warning from the 60's Generation," in *The Washington Post*, January 21, 2020; *The Next America: Boomers, Millennials, and the Looming Generational*

Showdown by Paul Taylor and the Pew Research Center (New York: PublicAffairs, 2014).

Details on early encounters between Obama and Biden also appear in Steven Levingston's rich and engaging narrative, *Barack and Joe: The Making of an Extraordinary Partnership* (New York: Hachette Books, 2019).

CHAPTER 2: WHAT IT TOOK

Jeff Connaughton relayed his impressions in his book, *The Payoff: Why Wall Street Always Wins* (Westport, Conn.: Prospecta Press, 2012).

Data and analysis on the Silent Generation appeared in Elwood Carlson's *The Lucky Few: Between the Greatest Generation and the Baby Boom* (The Netherlands: Springer, 2008).

For observations on evolving American notions of luck and will, I drew on Maria Konnikova's *The Biggest Bluff: How I Learned to Pay Attention, Master Myself, and Win* (New York: Penguin Press, 2020).

Biographical details in this and later chapters are drawn from interviews, and as well as from *Promises to Keep*, *What It Takes*, and Biden's second memoir, *Promise Me, Dad*. For the history of the Thomas hearings, I turned to *Strange Justice: The Selling of Clarence Thomas* by Jane Mayer and Jill Abramson (Boston: Houghton Mifflin, 1994).

CHAPTER 3: "GROW UP"

Biden's early comments and impressions in the Senate were captured in "Death and the All-American Boy" in *Washingtonian* magazine, June 1, 1974.

NOTE ON SOURCES

I benefited from an essay on Biden's inquiry by Roger Berkowitz, entitled "When Joe Biden Wrote to Hannah Arendt," published by The Hannah Arendt Center for Politics and Humanities at Bard College.

James Forman Jr. analyzed the politics of responsibility in *Locking Up Our Own: Crime and Punishment in Black America* (New York: Farrar, Straus & Giroux, 2017).

The accounting and examination of the phrase "through no fault of their own" appears in Michael J. Sandel's *The Tyranny of Merit: What's Become of the Common Good?* (New York: Farrar, Straus & Giroux, 2020).

Data on the growth of CEO pay in the years after 2007 was published by the Joint Committee on Taxation of the U.S. Congress.

CHAPTER 4: VEEP

Stacey Abrams explores the concept of the "new American majority" in her book *Our Time Is Now: Power, Purpose, and the Fight for a Fair America* (New York: Henry Holt, 2020).

For details on the arrangement of other vice presidencies, including Cheney's focus on the "iron issues," I benefited from Barton Gellman's *Angler: The Cheney Vice Presidency* (New York: Penguin Press, 2008).

Obama's use of empathy in political rhetoric is explored in an illuminating 2008 paper by Colleen Shogan, "The Contemporary Presidency: The Political Utility of Empathy in Presidential Leadership," *Presidential Studies Quarterly* 39 (2009): 859–77.

NOTE ON SOURCES

CHAPTER 5: ENVOY

Bill Bradley's recollections of traveling with Biden to the Soviet Union are drawn from Bradley's memoir, *Time Present, Time Past* (New York: Vintage Books, 1997).

In the summer of 2014, *USA Today* tabulated White House phone records and reported Biden's frequent contacts with officials in Iraq.

Biden's "bet" that Maliki would extend the Status of Forces Agreement was described in *The Endgame: The Inside Story of the Struggle for Iraq, from George W. Bush to Barack Obama*, by Michael R. Gordon and General Bernard E. Trainor (New York: Pantheon Books, 2012).

Zalmay Khalilzad and Kenneth Pollack assessed the strategic outlook for Iraq in their piece, "How to Save Iraq," in *The New Republic*, July 22, 2014.

CHAPTER 6: THE LUCKY AND THE UNLUCKY

Biden's assurance to Obama in 2008 that he would be too old to run for president appeared in Jonathan Alter's "Biden's Unified Theory of Biden," *Newsweek*, October 13, 2008.

Peter Beinart's piece on the potential value of a larger Democratic field in 2016, "Run, Joe, Run: Why Democrats Need a Biden Candidacy" was published in *The Atlantic*, May 9, 2014.

The details around Beau's death, and Biden's diary entry, appear in his memoir, *Promise Me, Dad*. Levingston's *Barack and Joe* provided valuable context on the final years of the Obama-Biden relationship in the West Wing.

Adam Entous's detailed, prescient account of how Hunter Biden's life could figure into presidential politics, entitled "Father and Son," was published in *The New Yorker*, July 1, 2019.

NOTE ON SOURCES

CHAPTER 7: BATTLE FOR THE SOUL

I benefited from reading an early edition of Samuel L. Popkin's book, *Crackup: The Republican Implosion and the Future of Presidential Politics,* slated for publication in 2021 (New York: Oxford University Press).

Lucy Flores published her account, "An Awkward Kiss Changed How I Saw Joe Biden," in *New York,* on March 29, 2019.

In March 2020, Renee DiResta, a researcher at the Stanford Internet Observatory, analyzed the effects of Jill Stein's promotion of #BidenCognitiveDecline.

Ryan Lizza assessed the divide between Biden and the young left in an insightful piece, "Biden Camp Thinks the Media Just Doesn't Get It," published by *Politico* on September 11, 2019.

Bernie Sanders reflected on his relationship with Biden in "Bernie Sanders Is Not Done Fighting," an interview with Andrew Marantz of *The New Yorker,* published June 9, 2020.

CHAPTER 8: PLANNING A PRESIDENCY

Biden's plans for early action were described by Matt Viser in "If He Gets a Presidential Day 1, Joe Biden Has a Nearly Endless List of Ways to Spend It," July 29, 2020, in *The Washington Post.*

Kevin M. Kruse explored the potential application of lessons from the Pecora Commission in "Why a Biden Administration Shouldn't Turn the Page on the Trump Era" in *Vanity Fair,* July 7, 2020.

I returned to Sandel's *The Tyranny of Merit* for a thoughtful exploration of changes in American conceptions of reward, control, and struggle.

ABOUT THE AUTHOR

Evan Osnos has been a staff writer at *The New Yorker* since 2008. His most recent book, *Age of Ambition: Chasing Fortune, Truth, and Faith in the New China*, won the National Book Award, among other honors. Previously, he reported from China, Iraq, and elsewhere for the *Chicago Tribune*, where he shared a Pulitzer Prize for investigative reporting. He lives with his wife and children in Washington, D.C.